Praise for
RAISE EARLY STAGE VENTURE CAPITAL

"When we launched our first fundraise I had zero experience in the art of raising capital. Looking back after reading this book—it answers all the questions I wish I had had answers to. Raising money is an art form and experience that like any athlete requires training and refining."

— **Alex Pall, The Chainsmokers & Mantis Venture Capital Founder**

"*Raise Early Stage Venture Capital* is an extraordinary guide for founders raising capital in Silicon Valley. I have been helping founders with this challenge for over 30 years, and this book provides the best, most comprehensive advice I have ever encountered. Hayley Leibson is a serial entrepreneur who has successfully raised money, and in the process gained extraordinary insights. She gives high quality "how-to" examples on topics ranging from how to apply to Y Combinator, how to reach out to investors, and what questions to ask them once you enter discussions. She discusses the benefits of sleep and exercise for better physical and mental health—which will make you more effective as an entrepreneur. I have read thousands of books in my career. *Raise Early Stage Venture Capital* is one of my top 10 books of all time. Buy it. Read it. Recommend it to aspiring entrepreneurs you know."

— **Tom Kosnik, Partner at FoundersX Ventures and former Stanford and Harvard Business School Professor**

"After I develop my billion-dollar idea and I'm ready to fundraise, this is the book I'm going into the meetings with. Well, I wouldn't bring it into the meetings because I wouldn't want the VCs to see it, but I would have all its learnings tucked in my brain."

— **Sarah Cooper, Comedian, Author of *How to Be Successful Without Hurting Men's Feelings*, and star of the hit Netflix comedy special, Sarah Cooper: Everything's Fine**

"The most practical, actionable, and immediately useful book on fundraising out there. It's full of plug-and-play templates, real-life examples, and practical advice for every step of your fundraising journey from founders who've done it. You'll have a much more successful fundraising experience after having read this book."

— **Lenny Rachitsky, Founder of Lenny's Newsletter and Podcast, Product Expert, and Angel Investor in Figma, Linear, Weblow, Substack, and more**

"All women teams raise roughly 2% of VC funds each year, and I love that this book makes startup fundraising more accessible for all."

— **Vivian Tu, Founder of Your Rich BFF, Personal Finance Educator, Creator, and Author**

"This book should be mandatory reading for early stage startup founders looking to raise money. Hayley skillfully breaks down the art of fundraising in a digestible, approachable and unfiltered manner while also providing major insights, tips and tricks on how the process really works. You will close the book feeling armed with the information you need, prepared for the process and ready to secure the bag. As she says, opportunity is not universal but this book will absolutely make it more accessible."

— **Jaclyn Johnson, Founder of Create & Cultivate and Investor in Away, Live Tinted, Ceremonia, Crown Affair, Chillhouse, and more**

"This is THE book I wish I had in-hand before doing an accelerator, raising a pre-seed round, and continuing to raise various rounds of venture capital. The entire fundraising process is a black box when you've never done it - mysterious, elusive, and fully gate kept - and pandora's box once the process begins - confusing, frustrating, and chaotic. Leibson's articulate and precise how-to is the only content I've ever read that addresses both of those realities. Leibson breaks down why to fundraise, how to fundraise, when to fundraise (as in, literally the best and worst months to ask for money!), and how to tell and sell your startup's story so you actually secure those checks. Not to sound shady, but there really are a ton of unspoken rules in Silicon Valley - more than I ever imagined. And now finally, someone in a direct, relatable and authentic way is removing the veil and telling all. Every single founder and aspiring entrepreneur looking to raise venture funding needs to read this book. There's nothing else to call it but a "secret weapon" - and I don't say that lightly."

— **Ali Kriegsman, Author and Exited Founder**

"*Raise Early Stage Venture Capital* delivers critical insights for how to successfully raise startup funding. It's chock full of essential strategies and tactics in one digestible and enjoyable book."

— **Nir Eyal, bestselling author of *Hooked: How to Build Habit-Forming Products***

"*Raise Early Stage Venture Capital* dismantles barriers for women and minority founders seeking early-stage funding. Through practical insights, Leibson navigates the complexities of venture capital, offering an inclusive and actionable roadmap for underrepresented entrepreneurs to thrive in a historically exclusive landscape.

—**Jaime Schmidt, Entrepreneur & Investor**

"Raising money not only requires great product, market and founders but those who succeed know the rules, tips and tricks, This book tells you how."

—**Steve Blank, Stanford Professor, Co-creator of the Lean Startup movement, and bestselling author of *The Startup Owner's Manual and The Four Steps To The Epiphany***

"Hayley has successfully raised tens of millions for her breakthrough startups, and this book shows how."

— **Jason Feifer, Editor in Chief, *Entrepreneur Magazine***

RAISE EARLY STAGE VENTURE CAPITAL

RAISE EARLY STAGE VENTURE CAPITAL

Hayley Leibson

JETPACK BOOKS

Published by Jetpack Books LLC
New York, San Francisco, London

First published in 2023.
Copyright © by Hayley Leibson.

The right of Hayley Leibson to be identified as the Author has been asserted in accordance with the Copyright, Design and Patents Act 1988.

Hardcover ISBN: 979-8-9895212-0-3
eBook ISBN: 979-8-9895212-1-0
Audiobook ISBN: 979-8-9895212-2-7

Designed by Diana Ang and Karina Granda.

All rights reserved; no part of this publication may be reproduced, stored in a retrieval system, or transmitted in any form or by any means, electronic, mechanical, photocopying, recording, or otherwise without the prior written permission of the Publisher. This book may not be lent, result, hired out or otherwise disposed of by way of trade in any form of binding or cover other than that in which it is published without the prior written consent of the Publisher.

Whilst every effort has been made to ensure that information in this book is accurate, no liability can be accepted for any loss incurred in any way whatsoever by any person relying solely on the information contained herein.

No responsibility for loss occasioned to any person or corporate body acting or refraining to act as a result of reading material in this book can be accepted by the Publisher, by the Author, or by any employers of the Author.

The Publisher does not have any control over or any responsibility for any Author or third-party websites referred to in or on this book.

For my parents and Sarah,
Thank you for your unwavering belief in me
and your endless love and support.

For Martin and Adrian,
I'm so grateful for every moment I have with you.
With all my heart, *ich liebe euch.*

Contents

Chapter 1	Introduction	15
Chapter 2	Preparation	27
Chapter 3	The Pitch Conversation	71
Chapter 4	Strategy	89
Chapter 5	Managing Yourself	115
Chapter 6	Common Mistakes	133
Chapter 7	Conclusion	139
Chapter 8	End of Chapter Summary Checklists	147
Chapter 9	Recommended Reading	153

Glossary	159
Notes	165
Acknowledgements	169
About the Author	173

"It is not the critic who counts;
not the man who points out how the strong man stumbles, or where the doer of deeds could have done them better. The credit belongs to the man who is actually in the arena, whose face is marred by dust and sweat and blood; who strives valiantly;
who errs, who comes short again and again, because there is no effort without error and shortcoming; but who does actually strive to do the deeds; who knows great enthusiasms, the great devotions; who spends himself in a worthy cause;
who at the best knows in the end the triumph of high achievement, and who at the worst, if he fails, at least fails while daring greatly, so that his place shall never be with those cold and timid souls who neither know victory nor defeat."

– Theodore Roosevelt, 26th U.S. President

Chapter 1

Introduction

Starting a company is a thrilling leap into an entrepreneurial journey, filled with boundless promise and inevitable hurdles ahead. It's an incredibly brave voyage into the unknown—fueled by vision and unyielding resolve to solve a problem that matters to build a brighter future.

The endeavor's significance cannot be understated, especially when one considers the monumental outsize impact of venture-backed companies on both the American economy and the world at large. According to a 2015 study by Ilya Strebulaev of Stanford University and Will Gornall of the University of British Columbia, 42 percent of all US company IPOs since 1974 were venture-backed. Venture-backed startups also represent 63 percent of the total market capitalization of public companies formed since 1974. Furthermore, specific to the impact on the US workforce, a 2010 study from the Kauffman Foundation found that young startups, most venture-backed, were responsible for almost all of the twenty-five million net jobs created since 1977.

If you want to quickly build a successful business that solves a problem on a global scale and become wealthy yourself in the process—access to venture capital is critical. While Silicon Valley proudly and loudly boasts that it's a meritocracy, data consistently shows venture capital funding being disproportionately allocated to startups led by a homogenous group of white, heterosexual men.

Historically, women and minority-founded startups receive a minuscule fraction of VC funding. As of 2020, for instance, women-identifying founders secured a mere 2.3 percent of the total VC invested in the United States. When it comes to racial disparities, Black and Latinx founders together received just 2.6% of VC funding in 2020. Over the past few years, the percentage of VC going to women and minority-founders rarely swings beyond 3%.

While venture capital funds and the industry have made lots of noise about investing in more diverse founders, these promises have yet to meaningfully change these depressing numbers. The process of fundraising is extremely unintuitive, critically important, and the know-how is difficult to learn because it's network-bound.

Through this book, I aim to demystify one of the most notoriously challenging parts of an entrepreneur's job—raising early stage venture capital. Our focus is solely on the process of raising early-stage venture capital with products that are pre-product market fit. This means you are just a person or team with an idea, or have a product that isn't showing hockey stick growth. You might have anecdotes and early signs of traction, but you don't have gobs of irrefutable data proving that customers are beating down your door for your product.

Why I'm a relevant source of advice:

Talent is universal, while opportunity is not. My entire career, I've been driven to broaden opportunities for women and minorities using technology to benefit humanity at scale. I believe now more than ever, the world needs products and services that meaningfully bring people together and increase empathy. We live in a network-bound referral-based society where people have the tendency to pattern match in ways that end up giving more opportunity and dollars to people with similar backgrounds. Most investing and hiring is sourced from personal networks, which excludes industry outsiders and underrepresented communities.

I've read so many entrepreneurial memoirs and business books, and while I enjoy the stories about people's lives, I often find them short on concrete, actionable guidance for achieving something specific in business like fundraising. After reading, I'm sometimes left inspired but with zero practical advice beyond generic maxims like "be your authentic self to succeed," "find your boss babe community of friends to support you," and "you need to hustle if you want to be successful!"

This book is a tactical unfiltered guide to help other entrepreneurs, specifically women and minority founders, raise venture capital for their businesses. I've now been lucky enough to be on both sides of the fundraising table—a feat that doesn't happen to most people with my background. My parents were extremely hard-working, and my family was not wealthy or well-connected. Prior to moving to Silicon Valley in 2016, my connections in the tech industry were nonexistent. I wasn't an alumnus of Stanford or an Ivy League institution, nor had I ever been part of a FAANG company or a high-profile startup. FAANG is an acronym for the five most prominent American technology companies: Meta (formerly Facebook), Apple, Amazon, Netflix, and Alphabet (formerly known as Google).

One of my first jobs in Silicon Valley was working as a marketing lead for Omidyar Network—a philanthropic or impact investment firm founded by eBay founder Pierre Omidyar. The VC partners I worked with at the fund spun out a new fund called Spero Ventures while I was working there. While my job wasn't an investor at the fund, I did get the incredible opportunity of learning what these VCs look for in founders' backgrounds, what the fundraising and due diligence process is like, how VCs support founders, and met a lot of venture capitalists and founders during my time there. My job was far from glamorous—it involved a lot of event planning, ordering food, and picking up trash after events but it was worth every late night and dirty napkin pickup.

Since then, I've started multiple venture-backed companies and as of this writing, my companies have raised over $30 million and are valued at over $130 million. Throughout my career, I've had to develop an extreme amount of grit, resilience, persistence, and determination to break into the technology industry and become one of the fewer than 2% of venture capital-backed women founders.

After my first venture-backed startup achieved a certain level of success and during a break between companies, I started angel investing in women and minority-founded consumer startups. In late 2022, I was included in a list of "Top Startup Founders Who Invest In Other Startups" by *Business Insider*. This book is an amalgamation of the fundraising advice I've given those and countless other startup founders, and guidance I wish I'd had when I was starting my first company. Before we dig in, it's important to make sure you are absolutely sure venture capital is right for your business.

> "The single most important contributor to a nation's economic growth is the number of startups that grow to a billion dollars in revenue within 20 years."
>
> – Carl Schramm,
> Economist and President of Kauffman Foundation

Should I raise venture capital?

If you decide to raise venture capital for your business, you should know exactly what you're signing up for, the pressures, and expectations. If you've picked up this book, you probably already decided raising venture capital is the best path forward for your business or you may be thinking about whether or not it's right for your business and want to learn more. Simply put, founders seeking venture capital aim to build multi-billion-dollar companies.

There is a wide spectrum of ways to fund your business including: using your savings, crowdfunding campaigns like Kickstarter, grants, convertible notes, venture debt, revolving lines of credit, or use your revenue to fuel growth. Venture capital is the most expensive funding option.

While most billion-dollar companies are venture-backed, it's only recently that businesses have been funded by venture capital at all. For hundreds of years, businesses were built on loans given by banks in exchange for interest. "By the 1960s and 1970s, venture capital firms were starting to form with the primary goal to invest in high-risk, high-reward technology businesses (at that time, mostly electronics and semiconductor companies)," states Ali Tamaseb, venture capitalist and author of the fantastic book *Super Founders: What Data Reveals About Billion-Dollar Startups*.

It's no surprise that creating a company worth billions of dollars is a difficult feat. Billion-dollar startups make up less than 0.1 percent of all startups. That's why they are often referred to as 'unicorns' because of their rarity—a term coined by venture capitalist Aileen Lee.

"Every company that a VC invests in needs to have the potential to return at least the fund. If you raise VC money, this calculation will determine the investor's expectation and will establish at what point they would be happy for you to sell the company."

– Ali Tamaseb,
Venture Capitalist and
Author of *Super Founders*

Before deciding to raise venture capital for your business, please read the expectations below and ask yourself and/or your co-founders if you have them: is this the type of business I want to run?

1. **You will build a multi-billion dollar business:** VCs are not looking for a multi-million or even billion dollar outcome—they want multi-*billion* dollar outcomes for their economics to work.
2. **Grow lightning fast or die:** Venture backers will expect you to scale up fast, hire quickly, and grow your metrics at an aggressive pace. Most VCs will place a lot of bets, and then double down on helping their portfolio companies that are performing well and let the others die.
3. **VCs may limit your flexibility to run your business the way you want to:** You are giving up ownership and control of your company when you raise venture capital. Some VCs will want to be heavily involved with the management of your company and potentially influence major strategic decisions and direction of the company potentially through legal force. Depending on your legal structure and agreements signed, they can even fire you.
4. **Focus on growth over immediate profitability:** VCs may pressure you to focus on growth sometimes at the expense of immediate profitability, making you dependent on further VC funding to stay alive.

Beyond Capital

Beyond cash in exchange for equity, VCs can bring much more to the table than just capital. Their value proposition extends far beyond funding and great investors can significantly impact the trajectory of a startup. Here is a shortlist of value VCs can bring to your business:

1. **Credibility and Branding:** Having top tier VCs or famous investors onboard instantly gives your startup credibility and elevates your brand within the startup ecosystem, in the eyes of customers, partners, and other potential investors. This makes it significantly easier to attract top talent and future investors onboard, bring onboard companies as customers if you are selling business to business [B2B], and your target consumer audience if you bring onboard Hollywood celebrity investors that are well-known to the public. Top tier VCs also make it easier to get press coverage for your startup.

2. **Talent Recruitment:** With their vast networks, VCs can help startups find and hire key team members through top of funnel, vetting, and even having dinner with candidates to convince them to join your company.

3. **Strategic Guidance:** VCs who were previously successful experienced founders and operators have seen numerous startups grow, pivot, succeed, and fail. They can offer strategic advice on the journey towards finding product market fit, customer acquisition, scaling, business strategy, and much more.

4. **Operational Expertise:** You can bring onboard VCs and investors with expertise in various parts of your business who can provide valuable advice along the way. For example, there are investors with deep expertise in the biotech industry, consumer packaged goods, beauty, etc.

5. **Mentorship:** Many of the best VCs act as mentors to founders, providing moral support, sharing experiences, and helping entrepreneurs navigate the extreme ups and downs of entrepreneurship.

6. **Exit Strategy:** Whether it's through an acquisition or an initial public offering (IPO), great VCs have the experience and networks necessary to helpfully guide startups through exit processes.

7. **Community and Learning:** As many founders know, entrepreneurship can be extremely lonely and isolating. VCs often plan events such as talks with industry experts, dinners, and retreats with companies in their portfolio to help founders build friendships and get inspired.

8. **Market Research and Insights:** VCs have a bird's-eye-view of various sectors, often seeing trends, threats, and opportunities before individual entrepreneurs might and can share relevant information with you.

9. **Fundraising:** VCs can provide introductions to other relevant investors (other VCs, angels, celebrities) and spend the time convincing other investors to come onboard to help with your current and subsequent fundraising rounds.

Introduction

What's in each chapter:

I recommend reading this book sequentially from start to finish. It's short and the concepts build on each other. If you'd prefer to skip around, here's a sneak peak of what's in each chapter and on deck:

- **Chapter 1: Introduction** — should your company raise VC, how VC companies impact the economy, and why I'm a relevant source of advice
- **Chapter 2: Preparation** — timing your fundraise, how to prepare, materials needed, startup accelerator programs, scam programs, finding people willing to help you, and outreach plug-and-play templates
- **Chapter 3: The Pitch Conversation** — mindset for success, how to craft and lead the pitch conversation, questions to be prepared for, questions to ask investors, how to present well, and what to do if the meeting goes south
- **Chapter 4: Strategy** — high-level strategy for executing a successful and quick fundraise, crowdfunding and non-accredited investors, founder etiquette, due diligence, meeting format, creating momentum, building your founder reputation and brand, and how to process and incorporate feedback during your raise
- **Chapter 5: Managing Yourself** — how to set yourself up for success mentally and physically for the fundraising sprint and marathon ahead of company building
- **Chapter 6: Common Mistakes** — common myths and mistakes to avoid
- **Chapter 7: Conclusion** — building towards a better future by solving meaningful problems and improving the numbers for women and minority founders
- **Chapter 8: End of Chapter Summary Checklists** — top takeaways and action items from each chapter
- **Chapter 9: Recommended Reading** — extremely useful books diving deeper into topics covered in this book and more
- **Glossary** — helpful terms referenced in this book and to know while fundraising

"The future isn't a place we are going to go, it's a place we get to create."

— Nancy Duarte,
American Writer and Businessperson

Chapter 2

Preparation

Tech news may bombard you with headlines proclaiming, "X Company Oversubscribed In 24 Hours" or "Z Company Raises $30 Million in a Week." However, beneath these splashy announcements lies the harsh reality: a 'successful' fundraise, like the ones making headlines, is the culmination of months of meticulous preparation. Make no mistake—preparing to fundraise is a rigorous, full-time job, demanding all of your attention in order to achieve success.

So, how do these high-achieving startups gear up? What essential materials should you assemble? Might it be beneficial to enlist professional help for your pitch deck? When is the optimal moment to kickstart fundraising, and what time commitment should you anticipate? We'll delve into these pivotal preparatory questions and more in this chapter.

Decades to Prepare: Individual Credentials

If you are a middle school, high school, college student, new college grad, or parent wanting to raise a child that was set up for the best possible chance of becoming a venture-backed founder—this section is specifically for you. This advice is for readers who think you may want to be a startup founder early in their career or in the future and have years with which to prepare for that potential career path.

You may know entrepreneurship is your path in life, and be ready to jump right in. There are many programs, and more popping up each year, that support young entrepreneurs, bypass traditional education routes, or offer non-traditional educational opportunities. The most well-known example of these programs is the Thiel Fellowship which is a unique program started by tech entrepreneur and VC Peter Thiel. At the time of writing this book, it offers young people under the age of 23 a grant of $100,000 over two years to drop out of college and start a company.

The idea behind the fellowship is to emphasize that traditional education isn't the only (or best) path for everyone—especially those with a burning passion or idea that can't wait. Thiel Fellow alumni include folks like Vitalik Buterin, Co-founder of Etherium, a decentralized, open-source blockchain system that features its own cryptocurrency called Ether; Laura Deming, the founder of The Longevity Fund, a venture capital firm that invests in biotech companies focused on extending human lifespans; and Dylan Field, Co-founder of Figma, a collaborative interface design tool. Other programs include the 20 Under 20 Summit, Echoing Green Fellowship, Kairos Fellowship, UnCollege, and Enstitute.

If you want to go to college and create the most VC-backable background for yourself, you could start by attending a university that is well-respected in Silicon Valley, is known for producing many entrepreneurial alumni, and from where many VCs themselves studied including places like Stanford, Harvard, MIT, or Wharton. Stanford alumni have founded companies including Google, Netflix, and LinkedIn. Facebook and Microsoft have roots at Harvard, although their founders didn't complete their degrees.

After graduating from one of these top institutions, you could get a job as an early employee as a software engineer or product manager at a fledgling startup that you believe has high growth potential and hopefully grows into an Airbnb, Uber, or Stripe-like scale while you're at the company. While working at a high growth startup, you would meet many people you may want to hire down the road or who may eventually angel invest in your company. You would attend networking events hosted by VCs to develop relationships with partners and let them know you are interested in starting a company someday. Once you find a problem and an idea you want to dedicate a decade plus of your life towards solving, you leave the high growth successful startup you joined and start fundraising.

Timing

Planning a successful fundraise involves seasonality. If possible, avoid fundraising between the months of June through August, and November through January. Wealthy angels and venture investors tend to be checked out during these times for summer vacations and winter holidays. You should either prepare and raise from September through the end of October, or from February through the end of May.

Another important element of timing to consider is when top startup accelerators demo days are occurring. We'll go more into detail about these programs later. If you aren't in an accelerator program like Y Combinator, it's wise to avoid two weeks before, and the week during Y Combinator's demo day. The reason being is venture capitalists and angel investors are scrambling to get into the hottest deals of the batch and recently the batch sizes or number of startups in each cohort has been increasing. Those factors may make it harder for you to get timely meetings and quick follow up meetings near Y Combinator's demo day.

It's critical to raise when you have a cushion of runway—the golden rule in the industry is about 8 months of runway. If you raise money when you are weeks away from running out of cash, you as a founder don't have leverage. The anxiety this may bring could shine through during investor calls and meetings, to your disadvantage. It may also affect your decision making—and cause you to bring onboard an investor that isn't the right fit for your company. The damage that might cause to your company could be severe and potentially kill the company.

Fundraising takes *a lot of time*, and time is your most precious resource as a founder. Creating a strong plan and doing all of the preparation required in advance, will increase the likelihood that you'll meet your goals by successfully raising the capital you need, and accomplishing that goal in as little time as possible. Preparation is everything. I've spoken with many founders who've 'winged it' with their fundraise—decided to raise a round, and each day of their raise researched new people to chat with and how to get warm introductions to those people. That is an extremely inefficient use of time, and will greatly lengthen the total length of your fundraise.

Taking a long time to fundraise is almost always deadly. The Silicon Valley investor community is relatively small, and as soon as you start reaching out to people letting them know you are "officially fundraising," word spreads like wildfire and your deal will be shared around. You'll be a ticking time bomb. It's part of your job as a Co-founder and/or CEO to secure the capital you need for your business, and if you don't do it in a timely manner, that signals to the venture community that you are incompetent as a founder—you weren't able to figure out how to raise, get in touch with the right people for your business, can't sell people on joining your business, and can't tell your story in a compelling way. All attributes that people look for when investing in a founder. If you aren't prepared, don't do your homework in preparation for your raise, the greater the likelihood that your fundraise will drag on and potentially be unsuccessful while signaling to the investing community that you are incompetent as a founder.

Because a long, drawn out raise sends bad signals to the venture community about your competence as a founder—it's critical that you prepare properly so that you can run a tight, efficient fundraise process. What does a tight fundraise timeline look like? Ideally, you are so prepared that you are able to get your round completely committed within the first 24 hours, or the entire fundraise wrapped up within a short 3-4 weeks. How long it takes to fill up your round will also largely depend on how hot the market is at the time you're raising. If the market is extremely hot when you start fundraising, you potentially may have your entire round committed in interest within 24 hours. In Chapter 3, I'll explain the mechanics of what you should say to an investor who wants to invest, and explain what "committed in interest" means and why you should use that strategy.

The current state of the economy, including the stock market, impacts both the amounts of capital invested by VC firms and on startup valuations. Typically during a bust economy, later-stage startups get hit harder and it's far more difficult for them to raise. Many VCs get especially excited to fund startups during bad economic times because some of the best startups were founded during recession including Apple, Airbnb, Square, Uber, WhatsApp, and many more.

Accelerators, Incubators, and Startup Programs 101

Accelerators like Y Combinator and many investors will advise you that there is no greater fundraising advice than building a product that customers love, growing month over month, and going after a massive market. Accelerators, incubators, and startup programs can be extremely helpful for securing funding and accelerating your company's growth.

Accelerators are typically short-term intensive programs (lasting months) and focus on iterating towards product market fit and funding, while incubators are normally longer-term programs. Programs can vary by sector like educational technology, gaming, food and beverage, biotechnology, etc. They can also vary by company stage and accept founders with an idea such as Entrepreneur First, or at various stages of the company's life through the growth stage.

There are hundreds of these types of programs in the United States alone, and more programs are popping up each year. There are even accelerators run by governments such as Start-Up Chile, an accelerator created by the Chilean government that welcomes startups all over the world. No matter which program you choose, it's critical to read the fine print and see if your startup will be required to be based out of any location or if there are any other strings attached that could impact your business.

The first accelerator program was Y Combinator, founded in March 2005 by Paul Graham, Jessica Livingston, Robert Tappan Morris, and Trevor Blackwell. Since then, Y Combinator has helped launch more than 3,000 companies including Airbnb, Stripe, DoorDash, Dropbox, Reddit, and more. Founder Paul Graham shared via Twitter on November 1, 2021, "Someone asked what the total value of YC companies was, so I tried calculating it. The current value of the top 30 is about $575 billion. When we started YC, I would have been astounded if you'd told me it would one day be $5.75 billion."

Since Y Combinator's founding in 2005, accelerators have exploded in popularity and as I'm writing this, there are over 500+ programs worldwide. According to Crunchbase, the top three accelerator programs based on successful number of exits include Y Combinator, 500 Startups, and Techstars. Today, you can find specialized accelerators—some are restricted to womxn-identifying-only founders, particular technologies, biotech, or social impact companies. Some accelerators provide collaborative in-person workspaces, industry event programming, and community building activities. There are also programs associated with education institutions like Stanford's StartX or UC Berkeley's Skydeck.

Accelerators like Y Combinator are particularly helpful in securing funding because many have a "demo day" or date during which you'll pitch your company to investors. There are many other accelerators that have copied that model, and also have demo days where you can pitch your startup to investor attendees either in-person or virtually.

Accelerator or startup programs with demo days can be extremely valuable for two main reasons. First and most importantly in my opinion, the demo day is a hard deadline in the mind of investors where they know you'll be sharing your startup with the world and accepting investment. Investors clamor to meet the best companies in the 'batch' before demo day actually occurs, to get the best deals. Programs are incentivized to tell startups in their batch to wait until very close to demo day or on demo day to start their fundraise because if all of their startups have already raised and closed their rounds, there would be no point to having investors come to demo day.

One important thing to note about programs with demo days—if you are unsuccessful with raising a round before or very shortly after demo day that will spook investors. They'll wonder why so much time has passed since demo day and why you haven't been able to close the round. Some investors have told me that if you are unsuccessful at raising your round near demo day, you may need to wait at least six months or a year before going back out into the venture ecosystem seeking capital. Therefore, to have the best possible shot of raising a successful round for your company if you're in an accelerator program with a demo day—you need to prepare for your fundraise (depending on how long the program is) before the program starts, and during the program as well as try to complete your fundraise *before* demo day.

Another benefit to having finished your fundraising goals by demo day is that you can share that with the press and hopefully get picked up in the media as "one of the hottest startups in the batch." With some accelerators accepting more and more startups into each batch, sometimes hundreds, it is becoming more and more difficult to stand out against the crowd.

In my opinion, the main reason to try and be included in media lists of the hottest startups coming out of the current program you're in, is because it can help you get in front of even more investors and get them to reach out to you if you're open to raising more capital in your round or are looking to add smaller checks with specific expertise. Another reason why you might want to be included in these media lists, is because you can then include those articles when reaching out to prospective hires to further increase your credibility and show that your early-stage startup is worth the career risk for folks who join.

I would argue that accelerator programs like Y Combinator specifically, are extremely valuable for business to business [B2B] founders—meaning founders whose startup sells to other businesses. The top accelerator programs have incredible alumni networks sometimes full of thousands of startups that may be potential customers in the future. A top accelerator brand like Y Combinator can also lend serious credibility to your company—helping you not only get Y Combinator alumni customers, but help you more easily get business customers due to Y Combinator's reputation.

At the time of writing this book, below is a shortlist of well-respected and well-known startup accelerator programs. I leave out the terms of each deal, as they change often for each program. It's worth noting—according to venture capitalist Tamaseb, "85 percent of billion-dollar startups did not go through any accelerator program. The ones that did—including Stripe, Airbnb, Coinbase, and Instacart—mostly graduated from Y Combinator."

Shortlist of Startup Accelerator Programs

1. **Y Combinator:** the first and most prestigious startup accelerator program based in Silicon Valley.
2. **University accelerator programs:** see if your university has an accelerator program and funding for startups. Examples include Stanford's StartX or UC Berkeley's Skydeck.
3. **Techstars:** three-month accelerator program hosted in a variety of locations in the US and around the world. Notable company alumni include SendGrid and Bench.
4. **500 Global:** accelerator program investing in early-stage companies across the globe. Notable company alumni include Canva and Udemy.
5. **Entrepreneur First:** accelerator program based in London that invests in individuals with a strong emphasis on pairing co-founders. Notable company alumni include Tractable and Magic Pony Technology.
6. **Corporate funded accelerator programs for startups:** Disney, Target, Sephora, Whole Foods, etc. all have startup accelerator programs.
7. **Government funded accelerator programs for startups:** Start-Up Chile for example.
8. **Arc:** Sequoia Capital's accelerator for pre-seed and seed-stage companies that includes an eight-week program for startups in the US and Europe.
9. **Surge:** Sequoia Capital's accelerator program focused on Indian and Southeast Asian startups.
10. **Start:** a16z's early-stage remote-first program open to startups across the globe.

11. **Sector specific accelerator programs:** an example includes a16z's accelerator for gaming companies called SPEEDRUN.

Example Accepted Y Combinator Application

I left Lunchclub to build a new startup called Neverland, and the company got accepted into Y Combinator, the most prestigious startup accelerator in the world. That company unfortunately failed. With permission from Y Combinator, below I share my application written for the company edited for brevity. While Y Combinator's application changes over time, I hope this real example of an accepted accelerator application is helpful.

Y Combinator Application:

1. If you have a demo, what's the URL? A demo can be anything that shows us how the product works. Usually that's a video or screen recording. (Please don't password protect it; just use an obscure URL.)

   Our product is currently under development, and we'll have a demo to share at the end of September.

2. Describe what your company does in 50 characters or less.

   A modern plant & gardening marketplace.

3. What is your company going to make? Please describe your product and what it does or will do.

   Neverland is making plants and gardening accessible to all through a modern, technology-backed marketplace. Buyers can discover new plants and gardening products, book gardening services online, and get inspired. Plant and gardening professionals can sell their products, connect with new buyers, and build their business.

4. Please enter the url of a 1 minute unlisted (not private) YouTube or Youku video introducing the founder(s). This video is an important part of the application.

   We shared our company URL here [now defunct]. It was a simple landing page with a waitlist.

5. How far along are you?

   We have been building the product since April, and are releasing our Testflight at the end of September for testing. We'll be releasing the product to the public at the end of October. We started conducting user research interviews in April and May (both buyer and seller sides). We created the product mockups in June and started development in July. We started conducting user research interviews in April and May (both buyer and seller sides). We created the product mockups in June and started development in July. We're releasing our Testflight at the end of September and launching the product in October.

6. How long have each of you been working on this? How much of that has been full-time? Please explain.

   Our Co-founding team has been working together full-time since January. Before then, Hayley made an early angel investment in her Co-founder's previous startup and they worked together in that capacity before joining forces full-time. Hayley previously Co-founded Lunchclub, the world's first AI superconnector backed by a16z, Lightspeed, and more now valued at $100+ million.

7. If you are applying with the same idea, did anything change? If you applied with a different idea, why did you pivot and what did you learn from the last idea?

   We have applied to YC with previous ideas and were asked last week after our interview with YC partners to submit a new application for our company Neverland. When we last applied to YC, we were considering experimenting with different ideas in the consumer packaged goods space. Upon early experimentation, we continued chatting with folks on our waitlist and realized that these consumers were interested in plants, growing their own food, etc. and had been facing an even more massive problem in buying, selling, and taking care of plants, herbs, gardens, etc. Given our extensive backgrounds in consumer tech and marketplaces and the outdated nature of the plant/gardening industry, we saw this as a massive problem and opportunity to tackle and modernize the $52 billion dollar market.

8. If you have already participated or committed to participate in an incubator, "accelerator" or "pre-accelerator" program, please tell us about it.

   N/A. Y Combinator is the only accelerator program we would consider.

9. Why did you pick this idea to work on? Do you have domain expertise in this area? How do you know people need what you're making?

   We picked this idea to work on because of a combination of factors: we deeply care about solving this problem and our backgrounds and experience in consumer tech and marketplaces.

   We know people need what we're making because of extensive interviews with both buyers and sellers. Sellers want to sell their plant and gardening products on a verticalized marketplace which doesn't currently exist, and there is a massive lack of trust on the buyer side—whether or not the seeds they buy are fake, whether plants will arrive in one piece, etc. Horizontal marketplaces like eBay, Amazon, Etsy, and others are incredibly vulnerable. Even though you can buy plants and seeds on eBay, Etsy, Amazon, etc. there is an unmet need: gardening buyers can't always trust that these horizontal marketplaces' supply are real (not a fake product) or will arrive in one piece. A lack of trust undermines any potential liquidity a big supply base creates.

10. What's new about what you're making? What substitutes do people resort to because it doesn't exist yet (or they don't know about it)?

    We're the first to build a marketplace in the extremely fragmented plant and gardening industry. Today, the process of selling and buying plants, seeds, and gardening equipment is broken. After talking with many people, we consistently heard how buying and selling plants and gardening products on horizontalized marketplaces like Etsy, Ebay, or Facebook Marketplace today is frustrating and a poor experience. Discovery and finding what you want is hard, there's a lack of trust on these platforms, and shipping is inconsistent. Plants and gardening are stuck where clothing was decades ago. Before Poshmark existed, you could sell clothing on Ebay and Etsy, however, the experience was fundamentally broken. Poshmark came in and created an amazing experience for clothes, and we're doing the same thing in the plant and gardening industry.

We're bringing tech into an outdated and extremely fragmented industry that hasn't seen innovation since the 60's. We've talked with many many plant owners and consistently heard how difficult it is to purchase and take care of plants. We're taking a modern approach by integrating technology throughout the entire purchase and care experience. We have several unique engagement mechanisms that bring our consumers back to Neverland through tech which we're happy to discuss over another call.

We're taking an extremely innovative approach in our business model by not taking transaction fees, but instead charging a protection/insurance fee per transaction. This came about because we've consistently heard from consumers we've chatted with that the trust in the purchasing experience around plants and gardening is broken. Consumers fear if the seed or plant they ordered is in fact real or if they're being scammed, if the product will arrive in one piece, and if they'll be able to get their money back if there are issues. We've decided to take this extremely innovative and unique approach by focusing our business not on transaction fees, but on insurance/protection fee to build trust while simultaneously incentivizing sellers to come to the platform because they get the best deal. We worked closely with our advisor/investor, the former COO of Walmart, to put our business model together. We've seen other companies in other verticals be successful in implementing this business model including the marketplace called Vinted. We believe that this will be a key lever for growth and building a trusted destination for all plant/gardening needs.

The substitutes people resort to now include large conventional superstores like Lowes and Home Depot; and horizontalized marketplaces like Etsy, Amazon, eBay, etc. The plant and gardening category has been exploding the last five years among millennial and Generation Z consumers, and they are the newest, largest, entrants into the category. This has only been accelerated by the pandemic. We've chatted with many folks on our waitlist, and they don't identify or want to shop at conventional superstores and they have a massive lack in trust in horizontalized marketplaces—in whether the product (seeds, etc.) they order are real or fake, whether a fully potted plant will arrive in one piece, etc.

11. Who are your competitors, and who might become competitors? Who do you fear most?

    Our competitors include the massive conventional superstores like Home Depot, and horizontalized marketplaces like Etsy, Amazon, etc.

12. What do you understand about your business that other companies in it just don't get?

    What we understand about our business that other companies don't get includes: (1) a unique business model informed by our deep understanding of both the buyer/seller problems in this space, (2) how trust for consumers is a massive problem and opportunity, and (3) using technology to solve this problem won't detract from people's experience of connecting with nature and will actually enhance accessibility to nature.

    As we shared above, we're taking an extremely innovative approach in our business model by not taking transaction fees, but instead charging a protection/insurance fee per transaction. We chose this direction because we've consistently heard from consumers we've chatted with that the trust in the purchasing experience around plants and gardening is broken. Consumers fear if the seed or plant they ordered is in fact real or if they're being scammed, if the product will arrive in one piece, and if they'll be able to get their money back if there are issues.

    We've decided to take this extremely innovative and unique approach by focusing our business not on transaction fees, but on an insurance/protection fee to build trust while simultaneously incentivizing sellers to come to the platform because they get the best deal. We worked closely with our advisor/investor, the former COO of Walmart, to put our business model together. We've seen other companies in other verticals be successful in implementing this business model including the marketplace called Vinted. We believe that this will be a key lever for growth and building a trusted destination for all plant/gardening needs.

    Many companies in this space take an active stance in technology because they believe it detracts from the experience of connecting with plants and nature. We have a contrarian belief due to our extensive user interviews and research—that millennial and Generation Z consumers, the biggest and newest entrants into the plants & gardening category, want a technology-backed experience and that makes plants and gardening accessible to more people and doesn't detract from connecting with nature.

13. How do or will you make money? How much could you make? (We realize you can't know precisely, but give your best estimate.)

71% of Americans participate in some form of gardening, plant, or lawn activity every year according to the National Gardening Survey. The plant industry is $52 billion, and here are our core assumptions about our business model below including our key monetization strategies that we worked closely with the former COO of Walmart to create:

- Buyer protection (transaction fee on buyer side): this will on average be 5% of the transaction cost. See Vinted as an example of this business model.
- Sponsored/Promoted Posts: sellers will be able to pay for sponsored and promoted posts. Costs here will vary depending on what the seller chooses.
- Buyer VIP membership: membership with select perks, expedited shipping, and discounts similar to Amazon Prime.
- Services: as we grow and expand, we will start offering plant/garden related services where we may take a transaction fee. Services can vary in price anywhere between 100-3000+ depending on the service.

As we scale, we can expand into additional categories such as: fertilizer, soils, microgreens, services, yard work, cannabis, pots/garden tools, yard/landscape equipment, etc. We expect buyers will purchase at least once a quarter if not every other month and will continue to do so year over year. Additionally, our customers will spend money on services and maintaining their plants and gardens (water, landscape, etc.). In order to make 100M GMV, we'd need 41K transactions a month or 500K transactions a year. The average LTV in consumer is 2 years and average spend per person in this vertical is upwards of $600 dollars annually according to the 2019 National Gardening Survey.

14. How will you get users? If your idea is the type that faces a chicken-and-egg problem in the sense that it won't be attractive to users till it has a lot of users (e.g. a marketplace, a dating site, an ad network), how will you overcome that?

    We created a waitlist three months ago and now have sub 15K folks on our waitlist.

15. What kind of entity and in what state or country was the entity formed?

    Delaware C Corporation operating in California.

16. List any investments your company has received. Include the name of the investor, the amount invested, the pre-money valuation / valuation cap, and the type of security sold (convertible notes, safes or stock).

    The startup is backed by a bunch of folks including fashion powerhouse Rebecca Minkoff and founders and executives from Glossier, Atoms, LVMH, The RealReal, Walmart, Target, Twitter, Brandless, and more. We're currently wrapping up our pre-seed round and raising on a SAFE.

17. How much money do you spend per month?

    15K per month.

18. How much money does your company have in the bank now?

    N/A

19. How long is your runway?

    14 months.

20. Please provide any other relevant information about the structure or formation of the company.

    Both Co-founders have equal equity in the company.

21. Are any of the founders covered by noncompetes or intellectual property agreements that overlap with your project? If so, please explain.

    N/A

22. Who writes code, or does other technical work on your product? Was any of it done by a non-founder? Please explain.

    The Co-founding team writes the code and does all of the technical work for the company.

23. Is there anything else we should know about your company? (Pending lawsuits, co-founders who have left, etc.)

    We had a YC interview last week.

24. If you had any other ideas you considered applying with, please list them. One may be something we've been waiting for. Often when we fund people it's to do something they list here and not in the main application.

    N/A

25. Please tell us something surprising or amusing that one of you has discovered. (The answer need not be related to your project.)

    Something surprising we discovered recently was the power of cold emailing. We've always been under the impression that it's impossible or at the very least incredibly difficult to get in touch with someone unless you have a warm intro. Through cold email, we were able to get a former COO of Walmart, former CEO of Brandless, and a former LVMH executive responsible for bringing Sephora to the United States all onboard as backers.

26. What convinced you to apply to Y Combinator? Did someone encourage you to apply?

    Y Combinator partners reached out to us at the beginning of last week, and we interviewed with Y Combinator partners last Wednesday 9/9. They asked us to complete this application after interviewing with YC partners.

27. How did you hear about Y Combinator?

    We've known about Y Combinator for many years, and it's the only accelerator program we would consider joining because of its fantastic reputation.

Beware of Scam Programs

Due to the increase of interest among the general population in 'entrepreneurship' and the glamorization of Silicon Valley by Hollywood, more and more people are interested in learning about this career path and whether or not it's right for them. More entrepreneurs and interest in entrepreneurship is a great thing for society, but there has been an explosion of scammers taking advantage of this newfound career path intrigue.

How do you know if a startup accelerator or program is legitimate? Here are a few red flags to look out for and information you should find out when evaluating startup programs and whether they are right for you—or just a scam.

Is the person trying to sell me this startup class or program on Instagram, TikTok, Youtube, etc. as an influencer?

There are too many social media influencers or modern day 'gurus' to count who host 'business bootcamps' or 'business vacays' where they encourage anyone (and everyone) to participate in an online program, or a short trip where you pay to fly and meet up with your new 'business besties,' get business advice, and get a chance to meet one-on-one with your business guru influencer (and get a photo op with them).

There are many people on the internet who've made it their career to coach others and host these business bootcamp trips, promising if you purchase their course or trip that they'll help your business reach certain revenue goals and milestones, or help you get your idea off the ground. Run for the hills and don't give them any of your money.

Does the program involve a lot of non-work-related activities, like spa time, massages, and driving fast cars?

Not joking—I've seen best-selling business book authors and famous entrepreneurs sell tickets to short week-long or even weekend-long business bootcamps where there are non-work-related activities like massages, test driving fast cars, and pool time on the itinerary. Legitimate startup accelerator programs will not have these types of activities on the calendar nor are they usually a week or weekend long. Well-respected programs often have occasional happy hours or dinners where you can meet other founders in your batch and talk about their startups. An important difference is that legitimate programs and VCs will not charge you anything if they offer any of these activities at events.

Does the startup program cost money to participate?

If the program is costing you money in order to participate, and it isn't a top well-known business school like Stanford University, University of California Berkeley's Haas, or University of Pennsylvania's Wharton, where you'll receive an actual degree, then it is probably not a well-respected program and not worth doing the course or potentially a scam.

Does the program invest in my company in exchange for equity?

If you aren't interested in pursuing a degree at a business school, and want to take your startup through a legitimate accelerator program—find programs that invest in your startup in exchange for equity in your company. If you plan to apply, make sure to check at the time of application what the standard deal is for the accelerator program you're applying to. Deals on offer sometimes change, and it's vital to understand the deal you may be accepting and what that means for your startup.

Is the program free?

If you're interested in learning more about entrepreneurship or what startup founder life entails, there are a few extremely high quality free online programs you can participate in. One of the best free programs is Y Combinator's Startup School—a free program through Y Combinator that gives you access to relevant and impactful curriculum, software that allows you to keep track of your startup's progress and keep yourself accountable, and other discounts and perks. They also have a free co-founder matching where Y Combinator will match you with co-founders based on your preferences for interests, skills, location, and more if you're interested in finding a co-founder.

All Raise, an organization that furthers diversity in entrepreneurship and venture capital, offers free online masterclasses. You can also find great content on YouTube and podcast platforms. I highly recommend searching for the following shows with content relevant to founders: Garry Tan,

Y Combinator, Lenny's Newsletter, Justin Kan, More or Less Podcast, Aarthi and Sriram, All-In Podcast, a16z, Talks at Google, 20VC with Harry Stebbings, Acquired, Levels, First Round Capital, No Priors, Kara Goldin, Computer History Museum, Stanford Graduate School of Business, TechCrunch, and Sequoia Capital, Greylock, Elad Gil, and Stanford eCorner.

How many other companies are in each cohort or batch?

An important factor into your decision should be how many other startups are admitted into the next cohort. As discussed above, if a cohort has many startups in the batch—that creates more competition around demo day fundraising and for press mentions. However, more importantly, more startups in a batch means less time and attention with the accelerator "partners" or folks who can offer you advice and help during your time in the program.

How strong is the accelerator's brand and network?

The brand of the startup accelerator matters. If the brand is strong—it can lend credibility to your startup and help get investors onboard, de-risk your company to new talented hires, help acquire customers if you're a B2B company, more easily get press, etc.

The strength of the accelerator's network is also a really important factor when choosing a program. All accelerators will tout that a huge value proposition of participating is the networking you get to do with folks in your cohort, and the network you then get access to after completing the program. A strong alumni network can help you conduct investor due diligence, secure partnerships, acquire customers, hiring and more.

So how do you find out the strength of an accelerator alumni network? Use LinkedIn to create a list of alumni to contact by searching for a mix of alumni (in your geographic region and beyond), who've participated in a recent batch, and who participated in batches years in the past. Send cold outreach to these people through email, social media direct messages, and LinkedIn requests. Introduce yourself, tell them you're considering joining the latest batch, and would greatly appreciate 5 minutes of their time to learn more about their experience in the accelerator program. If the accelerator alumni network is strong, some of those folks will respond and give you their time and feedback on the program.

Find People Willing To Help You

"Mentee" and "mentor" are words that make me cringe. They connote an antiquated, excessively formal transactional relationship where the "mentor" has valuable knowledge, connections, or status and the "mentee" is a sponge that merely receives.

Large corporations commonly have formal mentorship programs, but if you work for a fast-growing startup there will be no mentors. Whether you are an individual contributor or the CEO, it's your job to figure out what you need to learn, then find and convince people to help you.

Often you'll need to reach out to these strangers without a warm introduction from someone you know. So how do you convince a stranger to help you? The best and most meaningful "mentor" relationships are built on reciprocity and the belief that both parties have value and can help each other. Here is my advice for building this type of business relationship:

1. Create A Paper Trail On The Internet

It's critical that you have a paper trail on the internet, so that the person you're reaching out to can quickly verify you are a real person and not wasting their time. You'll have an even better chance of getting a reply if the person recognizes your face or name. Create and keep up-to-date social media profiles with a professional headshot of your face. Post content from these accounts over time. Make sure your following to follower count on these platforms is close to equal or that you have more followers so that people don't think you are a fake account.

Before you reach out to a potential mentor with an ask, authentically interact with them on social media. Did they publish an interesting blog article or Twitter thread recently? "Like" their work, comment with praise, or retweet a quote and tag them. Send the author a direct message letting them know you appreciate their work or opinions and why.

2. Outreach: Concise With A Clear Ask

You've ideally interacted online with your potential mentor over a period of time, built an internet paper trail to prove you're a real person, and are ready to reach out. Formulate a concise direct message or email briefly introducing yourself, include a clear call-to-action or ask, and the ability to opt-out.

Here's an example reach out template you could modify:

Hi Jane,

Happy Tuesday and hope you are having a great start to your week! I read your latest blog post on early-stage fundraising and found your advice incredibly helpful—especially your thoughts on how to design a great deck. My name is Hayley [link to LinkedIn], and I'm the founder of [X Company] and recent alumni of The University of Colorado at Boulder.

I would love to ask you a few quick questions about sharing a deck with investors. Would you be open to a brief 15 minute call anytime in the next few weeks? Happy to send over a calendar invite for whatever date and time works best for you. If now is not a good time, absolutely no worries, and please don't hesitate to reach out if I can ever be of help to you or your work. Thanks in advance for your reply, and hope to chat with you soon.

Warm regards,

Hayley

After you send this message, request to connect with the person on LinkedIn and include a note briefly introducing yourself and tell them you sent them a note and hope to connect with them soon. Wait a week before following up, and then follow up twice a week.

3. Offer Value

Before you have a call or coffee with a potential mentor, think through what you could offer them of value. Ask yourself: Can I teach this person something new about a space they are interested in? Can I offer to share their work within the various communities or newsletter lists I'm part of? Can I offer to connect them with specific talent they are looking to hire? Can I connect them with a company they would be excited to fund?

At the end of your conversation, ask if there is any other way you can be helpful to them and thank them again for taking the time out of their busy schedule to chat with you. If your potential mentor accepts any of your offers to help, always follow through. After your conversation, quickly follow up with a summary of what you discussed, any action items you agreed to, and thank them again for their time.

4. Always Conduct Double Opt-In Introductions

It's very important etiquette to learn early in your career that you should always conduct double opt-in introductions. A double opt-in introduction means that if you want to introduce people to each other, you need to ask each person for permission beforehand.

If you blindly introduce two people you know to each other, it's extremely off-putting and leaves the recipients feeling annoyed that you didn't consult them first, and they might not respond to the thread and lose respect for you. To ensure that doesn't happen, always ask both parties for permission to be introduced.

Materials

Fundraising takes all of your energy and focus. During fundraise preparation and execution, if you are doing a good job you will have no time for anything else besides hopefully maintaining your health.

Most accelerators and investors will recommend that only the CEO be pitching investors, and the rest of the team focusing on the product, customers, growth and retention during the fundraise. However, this is often not the case for a few reasons.

For my first venture-backed company, we found that it was far more efficient to have the executive founding team composed of the CEO, myself—the COO, and the CTO be part of the entire process and split the pitch threeways. Reason being, we were able to each share our part of the company and show investors that we were a great team, and we were all present to answer any questions investors had—leading to a much faster decision of yes or no. We also had other employees handling the business and technology while we were out fundraising.

While fundraising, I highly recommend setting up the company in a way with founding employees or contractors so that the business can continue running smoothly, and even continue growing instead of stalling while you are fundraising.

Here is a list of the materials you will need to prepare before you start (some of which you'll continue to iterate on while fundraising) which we'll dive deeper into below and in later chapters:

- ☐ Pitch
- ☐ Fundraising Tracks
- ☐ Outreach Tracking Spreadsheet or CRM
- ☐ Outreach Template Blurb
- ☐ Teaser Deck
- ☐ Full Deck
- ☐ Legal Paperwork
- ☐ Professional Team Headshots

The Deck

Many investors will ask for a deck, or funders you chat with will likely offer to share around your deck "to be helpful." Think about what can sell you and your company better—a couple of slides, or you animatedly selling your company's story to someone? It's the latter. Never say yes when someone asks to share around your deck and make it challenging for anyone to reshare it.

Create two versions of your deck: a teaser deck version and a full deck. If an investor requests to see your deck before meeting, share your teaser deck with them. The goal of the teaser deck is to get you from email or direct message to an actual meeting where you can sell the company and your competence as a founder. Therefore, the deck needs to be extremely bare bones and provide as little information as possible—give as few opportunities as possible to get rejected, and excite them enough to set up a meeting with you.

You don't want to appear weirdly secretive with your deck—but you do want to convey that you are extremely intentional with your time, respectful of other people's time, and expect the raise to wrap up quickly. Therefore, you are not open to being blindly connected to anyone on the planet who may be interested in investing. You want to be selective about investors you bring onboard, and only bring onboard people whose expertise you need, and want to work with.

If someone you are talking to over email or during a meeting asks whether they can "share your deck around their network" or "pass it along to someone" they think would be interested, what that can mean if you read between the lines is, "I don't have enough conviction to make a decision after this meeting with you. I want to run it by some of my friends, and if they think it's a good opportunity then maybe I'll invest." This is a sticky situation almost all founders have found themselves in, often more than once.

How should you address this? With grace, and by conveying that you aren't letting just anyone into the round. You could respond with: "Thanks for your kind offer to share [your company name] with others. I have a lot of conversations lined up, and expect the round to move really fast. Would you be open to sharing their names with me now or later over email? I want to be mindful of your friend's time, check out their experience, and make sure I'm not already scheduled to chat with them." Then if the funder does share the names, say you'll get back to them.

The golden rule to remember with introductions unless the dream investor scenario comes up like I described above—if someone offers to introduce you to other angels or VCs and they haven't invested themselves, respectfully decline. It's a bad signal if a VC or angel hasn't decided whether or not they are going to invest in your company, and then introduces you to another investor. Those two investors are going to invariably have a conversation where the other asks, "So did you invest?" and "Why not?"

What's the best method of sending a deck? You want to control who sees it, see if someone is passing your deck around, and get as much data as possible in the process. I recommend using a tool like Docsend, and create individual links for each potential investor that asked to see a deck. Also, require that people must input their email in order to view the deck so you can see if someone shares it around. Tools like Docsend are great to get additional information about how your deck is being received, even if there is little information—you can see how much time people are spending viewing each slide. Is there one slide people spend a lot more time viewing? It could be because most people find it confusing, or it could be because that's the strongest and most interesting part of your story.

Teaser Deck

As mentioned above, the teaser deck is a short version of your deck designed to get an investor to take a meeting with you—whether that be in-person, video, or phone call.

Here is what I'd include in a teaser deck:

- Slide #1: Company Name & Tagline
- Slide #2: Team
- Slide #3: Problem / Opportunity
- Slide #4: Market
- Slide #5: Why Now
- Slide #6: Solution (Your Product)
- Slide #7: Company name and CEO's email address

Example Teaser Deck

Here's the teaser deck I used for Astrapilot's pre-seed round.

Slide #1: Company Name & Tagline

Slide #2: Team

Founder & CEO

Hayley Leibson

- Co-founder & COO of Lunchclub AI, a16z-backed startup (2+ M matches globally, $100+ M valuation)
- Forbes 30 Under 30 Consumer Technology
- Y Combinator Alumni
- 10+ years of experience in consumer tech and AI
- Worked as a preschool + kindergarten teaching assistant throughout middle and high school

Slide #3: Problem / Opportunity

The Problem

$15K avg cost/year for preschool in the US

The extremely outdated and fragmented early childhood education industry is facing a crisis in three key areas: access, quality, and expense.

Millennials are now 90% of new parents and they care deeply about being good parents and seek digital solutions.

Slide #4: Market

The Market

Contrary to popular belief, early childhood education is a large market that is continuing to grow. Technology spend within ECE is growing faster than any other education segment at 20% CAGR.

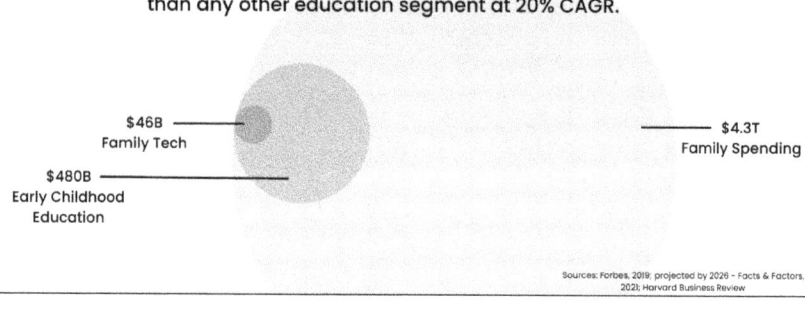

$46B
Family Tech

$4.3T
Family Spending

$480B
Early Childhood Education

Sources: Forbes, 2019; projected by 2026 – Facts & Factors, 2021; Harvard Business Review

Slide #5: Why Now

Why Now

Recent breakthroughs in large language models and deep learning have unlocked a whole new way for children to engage and interact with previously passive content, allowing for unprecedented engagement and retention outcomes.

For the first time in history, affordable 1:1 education is possible at-scale and personalized learning is truly possible due to more data and highly customizable experiences driven by AI.

Slide #6: Solution (Your Product)

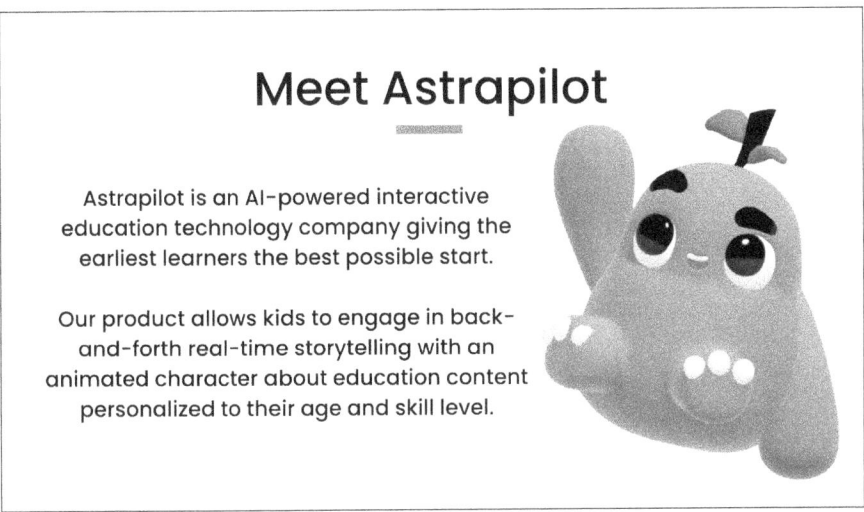

Slide #7: Company name and CEO's email address

Full Deck

Here is what I'd include in a full deck:

- Slide #1: Company Name & Tagline
- Slide #2: Team
- Slide #3: Problem / Opportunity
- Slide #4: Solution (Your Product)
- Slide #5: Why Now
- Slide #6: How It Works (how your product or service works)
- Slide #7: Defensibility
- Slide #8: Traction
- Slide #9: Vision Statement
- Slide #10: Company name and CEO's email address

Example Pitch Deck

Here's the pitch deck that helped my first startup Lunchclub raise millions to help build the professional network platform of the future (some sensitive data is redacted):

Slide #1: Company Name & Tagline

Preparation

Slide #2: Team

Slide #3: Problem / Opportunity

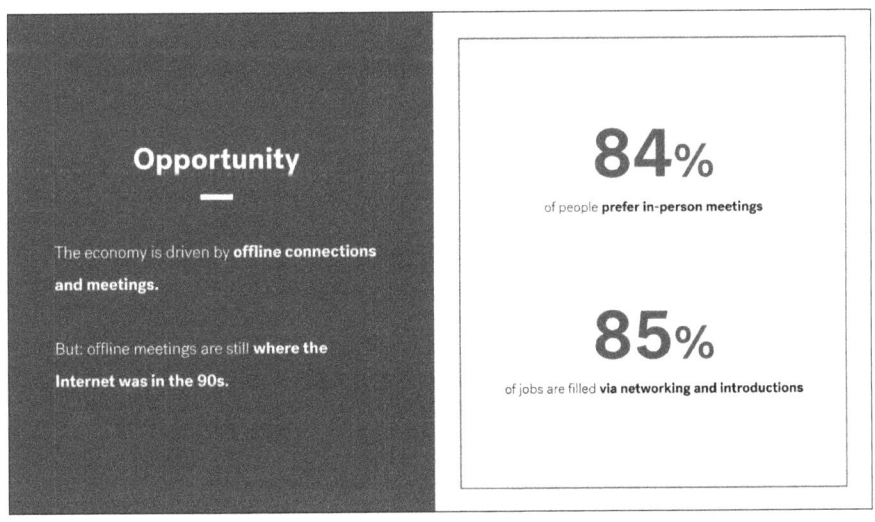

Slide #4: Solution (Your Product)

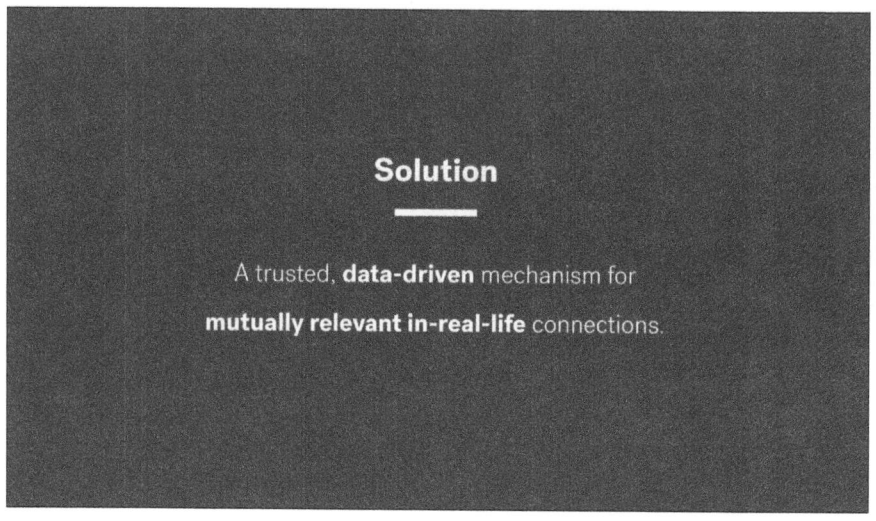

Slide #5: Why Now

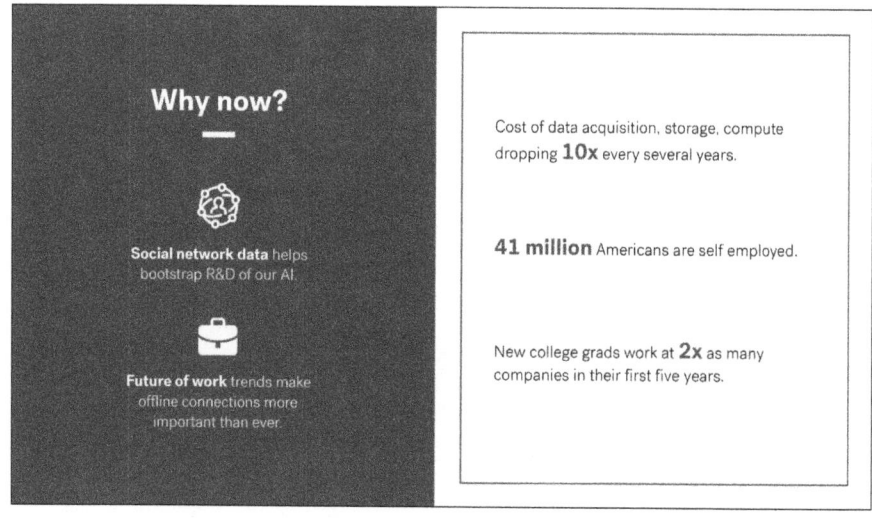

Preparation

Slide #6: How It Works

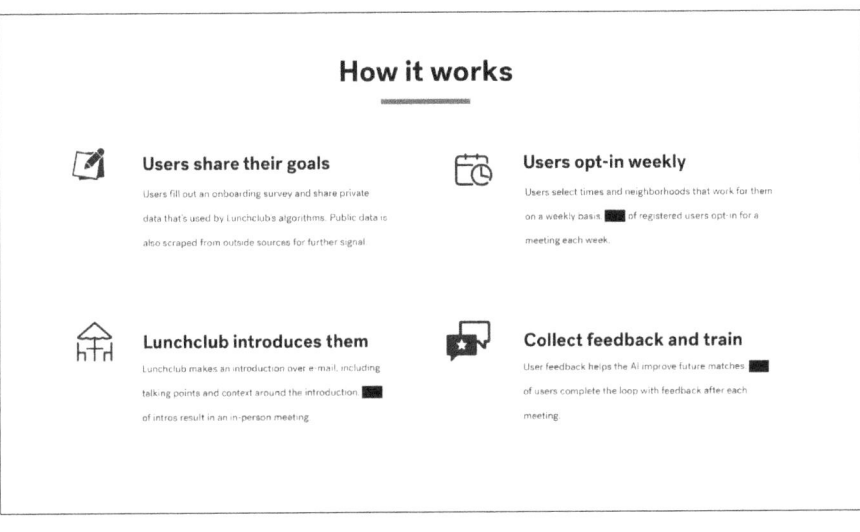

Slide #7: Defensibility

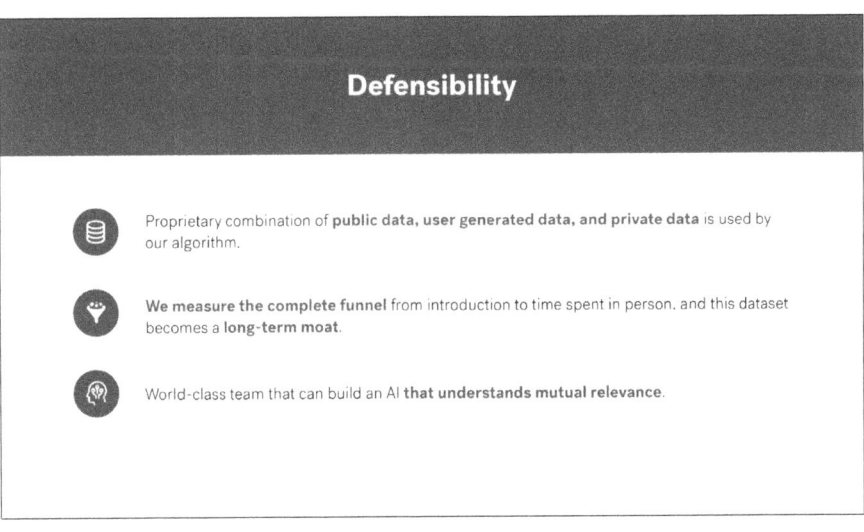

Slides #8-11: Traction

Virality and network effects

Natural global network effects: professional connections span multiple cities

19% (and growing) of users were invited by **someone in another city**

> If Lunchclub no longer existed, a huge part of my life would be missing.
> — Helen Jiang, **Stanford researcher**
>
> Lunchclub outsources my networking and advanced my goals in ways that feel authentic.
> — Madeline Lauf, **Village Global founder**

Engagement and retention

The average user takes **10 meetings a year**. This is an order of magnitude higher than "swiping" networking apps and LinkedIn.

Consistent engagement across later cohorts and new cities since launch.

In a recent survey, 42% of users would be **very disappointed** if Lunchclub went away.

Kong funds Natalie's animated series

Kong (YC founder) invested in Natalie's animated series in Los Angeles.

> " I've had an idea for an animated series for a while. I got a production company on board after putting a pitch deck and pilot script together. I then showed the deck to my Lunchclub connection, Kong, and he said 'I would love to fund this.'

Sam and Annie become co-founders of Lexi

Samuel and Annie met through Lunchclub and became co-founders of Lexi, an AI-powered language tutor.

> " A friend recommended Lunchclub as a way to expand your network and meet people who could become advisors, mentors, and potentially a co-founder. I was skeptical at first...[but] Annie fit every bucket I could have possibly imagined for a cofounder.

Slide #12: Vision Statement

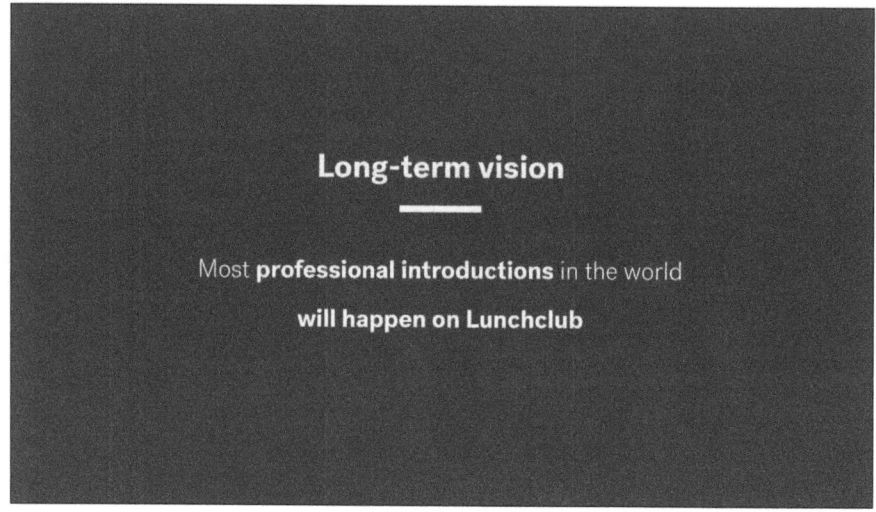

Slide #13: Company Name [individual contact information redacted]

For more examples of pitch decks, check out *Insider's* Pitch Deck Library where you can search and view over one thousand pitch decks that startups including Lunchclub, Uber, Airbnb and more used to raise millions of dollars from investors. *Insider* frequently publishes new pitch decks and their library includes startups from pre-seed to growth stages. You can search for decks by startup name, funding stage, and even geographic region.

How to Get Inbound Outreach & Pre-qualify Investors

How can you generate interest and investors reaching out to you before you have a product in the market? In startupland, before founders announce their company name and specifics about what they are building on their social media profiles—they update their headers and workplace to "Stealth" or "Stealth Company."

VCs are constantly scouring LinkedIn specifically to find profiles of great-looking founders-to-be and get into the round early. To strengthen the quality of the inbound you'll receive by updating your profile that you're working on "Stealth," add a short one sentence description about the sector you are building in. That way, you get investors reaching out who are relevant to you and actively invest in your sector (biotech, consumer, etc.).

Here are a few examples of potential descriptions:

- Building a B2B product in life sciences.
- Building something new in the creator economy space.
- Reimagining education for the modern toddler.
- Working to make nutrition accessible to the masses.

When investors start reaching out to you, it's helpful to ask them a few questions in advance of agreeing to a call or meeting so that you can make sure it's a potential fit for both you and the investor. Sometimes people don't advertise on their profiles that they actively angel invest, and if you receive an inbound note that's confusing—it's worth clarifying. It's also become very in vogue and a status symbol for people to advertise on their social media profiles that they angel invest, even if they don't or have only done so once twenty years ago.

You can Google an angel investor's name and see if they are frequently or recently included in articles announcing company fundraises or search for them in places like Pitchbook or Crunchbase to see if they are listed on many cap tables. If not, it's worth asking some of these pre-qualification questions to save yourself time. Below is a template you can use followed by examples:

Pre-qualify Template:

Hi [Investor First Name],

Thanks for reaching out! [Compliment an investment they made, a recent blog post they've written, or mention a portfolio company achievement]. Just to clarify, are you interested in chatting from an investing perspective? If so, I want to be mindful of your time—do you invest in pre-revenue biotech startups?

Thanks,

Becca

Pre-qualification Response Examples:

Hi Amy,

Thanks so much for reaching out and for your kind words! I'm a huge fan of your investment in Athletic Greens. Are you interested in chatting from an investment perspective? I want to be mindful of your time—do you invest in pre-seed/pre-launch consumer technology companies?

Warmly,

Hayley

Hi Molly! Thanks for connecting and for your kind note! I'm friends with [NAME] and would be really excited to chat with you specifically about Astrapilot. To be respectful of your time before scheduling a call, I'd love to understand:

What's your ideal check size when you invest?
Do you invest personally or through a syndicate?
What were your last few investments and when were they made?

Thanks in advance for your reply!

Investor Outreach Templates

Approximately 2 months or more before you actually *start* fundraising, you will need to start outreach to investors and get meetings on your calendar. In order to achieve momentum, you need to fill up every available spot for the few week fundraising sprint.

Outreach Template to Venture-Backed Founders

You know the person:

Subject Ideas:

- If you haven't spoken to someone in a long time:

    Hope You Are Well! | [First name of the person you haven't spoken to in a long time] (Company Name) <> Hayley (Astrapilot)

- The contact is a good friend or acquaintance:

    👋Virtual coffee chat this week? | [First name of good friend or acquaintance] (Company Name) <> Hayley (Astrapilot)

Body:

Hello Valerie,

I hope you are well! [personal note + potentially mention where you last saw each other or chatted about.]

Last time we chatted I mentioned my startup Astrapilot, the world's first AI-powered preschool educator. I'm working to solve a problem I experienced first-hand in the early childhood education space utilizing my expertise in AI and consumer tech. I'm a Forbes 30 Under 30 for consumer tech, YC alum, and previously Co-founded a16z-backed Lunchclub AI—the world's first AI superconnector utilizing LLMs to match millions of young professionals worldwide resulting in jobs, mentorship, friendships, and more.

We're interested in bringing onboard investors that you've worked with and would greatly appreciate a quick ten minute call to get your thoughts on a few folks. Would you be available for a brief call [Monday 12/14 at

1 PM or 2 PM PT]? *Happy to send over a calendar invite, and looking forward to chatting with you!*

Warmly,

Hayley

Cold Outreach Template (You've Never Met The Investor)

Subject Ideas:

- If you don't have any strong mutual connections with the person, mention any brand-name previous companies, universities, or accolades:

  👋 Marissa <> Hayley (Stealth, Forbes 30 Under 30)

- You have strong affiliations with the investor's background (you studied at the same university, came from the same city or town, both enjoy ABBA or reading SciFi, you previously worked at a company they invested in):

  👋 Tammy <> Hayley (CU Boulder Alum, Ex-Apple & Amazon)

- If you share strong mutual connections with the person:

  👋 Holly <> Hayley (Friends of Rebecca Edwards & Ali Blake)

Body:

Hello Valerie,

I hope you are healthy and doing well! If you're open to connecting at this time, I'd love to share the work that we're doing.

My name is Hayley, and I'm a Forbes 30 Under 30 2020 for consumer tech and prev. co-founded an a16z-backed startup called Lunchclub AI—the world's first AI superconnector utilizing LLMs to match millions of young professionals worldwide resulting in jobs, mentorship, friendships, and more. I'm now working on something new to solve a problem I experienced first-hand in the early childhood education space utilizing my expertise in AI and consumer tech.

I'd love to chat sometime early next week if you're interested in this problem space. Would you be available for a brief call [Monday 12/14 at 1 PM or 2 PM PT]? Happy to send over a calendar invite, and looking forward to chatting with you!

Warm regards,

Hayley

You know the person:

Subject: Hope You Are Well! | Valerie (Angel) <> Hayley (Stealth Co)

Hello Valerie,

I hope you are healthy and doing well! [Share background context here to remind the person how you know each other.]

Last time we chatted I mentioned my startup Astrapilot, the world's first AI-powered preschool educator. I'm working to solve a problem I experienced first-hand in the early childhood education space utilizing my expertise in AI and consumer tech. I'm a Forbes 30 Under 30 for consumer tech, YC alum, and previously Co-founded a16z-backed Lunchclub AI—the world's first AI superconnector utilizing LLMs to match millions of young professionals worldwide resulting in jobs, mentorship, friendships, and more.

I'd love to have a brief phone call if you're interested in what we're building with Astrapilot! We'll be raising our seed round in the new year. If not, no worries, and please let us know if I can ever be of help.

Warm regards,

Hayley

Legal Preparation And Paperwork

Before you begin your fundraise, you will need to set up your company so that it is ready to receive investment. We're so often focusing on building, it can seem like a waste of time and even a buzz kill to prepare for what can go wrong in the future. However, over the course of starting companies and advising many others, I can't stress enough the importance of setting yourself up personally to weather often unforeseen and painful challenges.

Most founders, myself included, are optimists by nature. The odds of success are stacked against us—more than two-thirds of startups fail, according to the Harvard Business Review. Still, despite the odds, we risk everything from financial stability to health to make something people want.

Founders start companies planning to dedicate 10-plus years of their lives to the business, longer than the duration of the average marriage in the United States. You will spend most if not all of your waking hours on your company, and probably spend more time with your co-founders than anyone else in your life. Since Silicon Valley is the epicenter of ridiculous wealth creation, it tends to attract short-term opportunists and fraudsters looking to make a quick buck.

When you enter into any kind of business relationship—whether it's co-founders, investors, or partners, you need to trust but verify from day one. Reach out to founder friends you trust, or reach out to founders you respect who are strangers, and ask for referrals to lawyers with employment and corporate expertise.

To protect all of the hard work and time put into your startup, even if you are CEO, you need to hire a personal lawyer with employment and corporate law expertise to review your employment contract, the company's bylaws, articles of incorporation, among other important documents. The company's lawyer has the startup's best interests in mind, not yours. Hiring your own counsel is invaluable in helping you protect your stock and mitigating potential future legal issues.

The ousting of co-founders is shockingly common in Silicon Valley. When startups start becoming successful even at the earliest stages, people get greedy and fire their co-founders for a larger share of the pie. There is a particularly egregious type of ousting that's not publicly talked about because of founders signing nondisclosure agreements or "gag orders." Through startup whisper networks, many share the opinion that women, minorities, and founders from low socioeconomic backgrounds disproportionately suffer from these immoral power grabs.

Too often, founders are told the sexist conventional wisdom that they must have a co-founder to raise venture capital. The reasoning is that startups are extremely difficult and you need someone with a complementary skill set who is as dedicated as you are to help make the company a success.

However, you should never start a business with someone you don't deeply trust—hopefully it should be someone you've worked with in the past or went to school with, and ideally have known for at least a decade. This co-founder bias is a huge obstacle for people from less privileged backgrounds, because the tech industry is overwhelmingly male and white. Founders feel they are forced into these co-founding relationships with people they believe have complementary skill sets, but they barely know. It's a recipe for disaster.

I've heard many deplorable stories about founders adding a person of color or woman to their founding team so they can more easily raise money from diversity-focused venture capital funds, only to oust the diverse founder shortly after their fundraise.

When a founder is being ousted, they are presented with a separation agreement, nondisclosure agreement, and typically a cash offer for signing and giving their equity back to the company, and told to sign immediately or given a tight deadline. If you don't readily have a few thousand dollars available to pay a lawyer hourly to help you navigate the situation, you may sign a terrible agreement not knowing what options for recourse are available to you. If this worst case scenario happens to you, know that you are not under any real time constraint, and don't sign anything until you have legal representation.

Outside of hiring a lawyer to set up your legal paperwork with your personal best interests in mind, you'll need legal help to form an appropriate legal entity in order to enable venture-backed investment. Most U.S. investors prefer investing in Delaware C-corporations, and some can only invest in that company structure. I recommend hiring a different lawyer to handle company matters, or using a service like Clerky or Stripe Atlas to quickly and cheaply get all of your legal paperwork done.

Chapter 2: Preparation
End of Chapter Summary Checklist:

Here is a shortlist of the materials you will need to prepare before you start (some of which you'll continue to iterate on while fundraising):

- ☐ Pitch
- ☐ Fundraising Tracks
- ☐ Outreach Tracking Spreadsheet or CRM
- ☐ Outreach Template Blurb
- ☐ Teaser Deck
- ☐ Full Deck
- ☐ Legal Paperwork
- ☐ Professional Team Headshots

What information to include in a teaser deck:

- ☐ Slide #1: Company Name & Tagline
- ☐ Slide #2: Team
- ☐ Slide #3: Problem / Opportunity
- ☐ Slide #4: Market
- ☐ Slide #5: Why Now
- ☐ Slide #6: Solution (Your Product)
- ☐ Slide #7: Company name and CEO's email address

What information to include in a full deck:

- ☐ Slide #1: Company Name & Tagline
- ☐ Slide #2: Team
- ☐ Slide #3: Problem / Opportunity
- ☐ Slide #4: Solution (Your Product)
- ☐ Slide #5: Why Now
- ☐ Slide #6: How It Works (how your product or service works)
- ☐ Slide #7: Defensibility
- ☐ Slide #8: Traction
- ☐ Slide #9: Vision Statement
- ☐ Slide #10: Company name and CEO's email address

Chapter 3

The Pitch Conversation

Pitching IRL (in real life) couldn't be more different than what's depicted on television shows like shark tank or dragon's den. In those television show scenarios, the venture capitalists hold all of the power. The entrepreneur is confidently sharing their 5-minute pitch, nervously fields questions from investors, and begs one or all of them to invest. In reality, raising money is completely different and requires a complete mindset shift.

It may appear as though investors hold all of the cards because they have money, but in actuality, you as the entrepreneur hold the power. You are the one who is responsible for 100xing the investors investment and making them and their LPs rich. Day after day, you as the entrepreneur will be working away making your business a financial success for the investor. It is an absolute privilege for the investor to have your time, and for the opportunity that you'll even consider accepting their investment. It's a once-in-a-lifetime opportunity for any venture capitalist or angel to invest in your company, and join you for this ride.

This doesn't mean you ever have the permission to be an asshole, like the entrepreneurs depicted in the massively successful HBO television show *Silicon Valley*—when the founders of the hot startup Pied Piper shift their mindset realizing they hold the power, and treat investors poorly.

When you pitch an investor, it's your job to ask them questions and suss out whether or not you are interested in working with them, just as they are asking you questions to decide whether or not they want to invest in you.

Learn and Use Lingo

One time in the past, I had a pitch conversation with a female venture capitalist that I really respected. I read all of her work, listened to all of her podcast episodes, and knew she was wicked sharp and I was so excited to have a meeting with her. Whether or not she chose to invest didn't matter to me—it felt like an incredible honor and opportunity to get her thoughts on what I was building. If she chose to invest, that would just be an unbelievable bonus.

During my meeting with this female venture capitalist, I shared who I was, what I was building, and then we quickly dove into rapid fire questions. She asked me what my "take rate" was. I had no idea what that meant, so I asked her the definition. She said it meant what percentage I make in profit from a sale. It became quickly apparent that she wasn't impressed and was surprised that I didn't know that term. She didn't invest, but I greatly appreciated her explaining that term, among others to me. I made sure to learn as many business school and VC terms that I could that I thought could apply to my specific business, or any business in general at my stage.

How To Set Up The Meeting

Bring the energy. If you aren't excited about what you're doing—who else would be? Get in the right frame of mind. It will be tedious, hearing the same questions over again, saying the same thing over and over again, but you need to bring positive upbeat energy every time. It's your job.

Example first meeting or call script:

Hello [First name]! Happy Tuesday and hope you're doing well and having a great week! Any highlights so far from this week?

Anchor the investor so they are in a positive frame of mind:

Anchor the investor at the beginning of the call by making them bring up something positive. Questions like, "What's been a highlight of your week thus far?" or "Before we jump in, what's been really exciting to you recently?"

Compliment their work and share why you are excited to speak with them specifically, mention any connections/social capital:

Excited to connect with you and share what we are building with [your company name.] Compliment their work or recent news. I really enjoyed your recent blog post about X, and respect your deep expertise in Y, Z, K. or "I love a lot of companies you've invested in including Hipcamp. I've been a customer for many years, and love the product."

Before jumping in, I've done a lot of research on the fund—but was hoping to ask you a few quick questions if that's okay?

1. Is your normal check size $25K? Or what is your normal check size?
2. Do you have any ownership requirements?

3. How does your process work and what does your decision-making timeline look like? Can you make a quick decision, or do you need to go through an approval process? What is that approval process?

Template Pitch

After setting up the conversation above, here is a template pitch you can use to craft your own:

1. **Introduction:**
   - Introduce yourself, sharing your background, and why you are the right person to build this company.

2. **The Problem:**
   - Articulate the problem you are trying to solve, how you encountered it, and how many people have this problem (the market).

3. **Your Solution (Service or Product):**
   - Share a clear one-liner about what your product is or will be, and then share more about how it works from the user's perspective.

4. **Why Now:**
   - Why this exact moment in time has unlocked this opportunity. Is there a breakthrough new technology that allows this problem to be solved now, when it hasn't been able to be solved in the past? Is there a major societal shift in behavior or change in government laws?

Example Pitch: Astrapilot

Here is the pitch I created to raise funding for my startup Astrapilot using the template above:

1. **Introduction:**
   - I'm a Forbes 30 Under 30 for consumer technology, Y Combinator alumni, and previously Co-founded and served as Chief Operating Officer of a16z-backed superconnector product Lunchclub AI, which to-date has matched millions of young professionals globally resulting in jobs, mentorship, and more.

2. **The Problem:**

    - After becoming a mom last year, I started looking into early childhood education options for my son. I joined parenting communities IRL and online searching for options. I discovered that the early childhood education industry is extremely outdated and fragmented, and is facing a crisis in three key areas: access, quality, and expense.

    - Access: In terms of access, teacher vacancies are reaching crisis levels in the US, and I was shocked to find out that only 50% of children in this country receive any kind of formal early childhood education before the age of 5.

    - Quality: Second, in terms of quality—basic numeracy and reading levels are in the steepest decline in more than 30 years. Schools are even loosening basic teaching requirements to fill gaps due to teaching vacancies, and quality is continuing to decline.

    - Expense: Meanwhile, education is more expensive than ever. Early childhood education, even at this early stage, is typically families' first or second largest expense after their mortgage or rent costing an average eye-gouging price of $15,000 nationwide per year.

    - Why does this matter? 90% of the human brain develops before age 5, and achievement gaps open up well before kindergarten. Quality and accessible early education is critical in shaping our future society.

3. **My Solution / Product:**

    - We're working to solve this problem at Astrapilot by building an AI-powered educator that allows kids to engage in back-and-forth dialogic learning with an animated character personalized to their age and skill level.

4. **Why Now:**

    - Recent breakthroughs in large language models (e.g. ChatGPT) are enabling a whole new way for children to engage and interact with previously passive content, allowing for unprecedented engagement and retention outcomes. For the first time in history, affordable 1:1 education is possible at-scale and personalized learning is truly possible due to more data and highly customizable experiences driven by AI.

Fundraising Tracks

Fundraising tracks are rabbit holes you'll go down during conversation about various parts of your business such as questions about traction, go-to-market, business model, and more specific to your sector (consumer, B2B, social products, etc.). It's extremely helpful to think through what questions you'll likely be asked by investors, especially the challenging ones, and prepare clear concise answers beforehand. This will help you appear more confident during your meetings.

Once you start fundraising, you'll quickly see patterns of questions emerge after a few meetings. These patterns show what investors believe to be the biggest risks of your business. During meeting breaks, you should continuously iterate and improve upon those answers if they keep popping up.

If you don't have a product in the market yet, it's important to know what metrics you'll use to measure your company's performance. If your product is in the market, you should know your numbers. Below are some general questions you'll likely be asked by investors and examples of questions sector specific. Most companies' north star metric is revenue, and there are different ways of measuring that depending on the sector.

General Questions

1. How much are you raising and at what valuation?
2. How much have you raised to-date and from whom?
3. How are you structuring this round?
4. What are you looking for in an investor?
   Why do you want to partner with us?
5. What is defensible about your product or service?
6. Who are your main competitors?
7. What traction do you have?
8. How do you plan to get customers?
   What's your go to market strategy?

9. How did you land on this particular product as a solution?
10. What milestones will you achieve with this raise?
11. What are your hiring plans?
12. What are the biggest hurdles ahead for your business? How could you fail?
13. What's the greatest challenge you're facing right now?
14. How many customers or users do you have?
15. What is your product roadmap?

Specific Sector Questions

- Consumer Businesses:
    - What is your revenue? (either monthly revenue, monthly recurring revenue if you sell a consumer subscription, or gross merchandise volume)
    - What does retention look like?
    - How many active users do you have?
    - What is your customer acquisition (CAC) cost? How will that change over time?
    - What's your CAC payback period?

- Enterprise Businesses:
    - What's your revenue or annual recurring revenue?
    - How many paid pilots have you done?
    - What companies have participated in your pilot?
    - How many LOIs, or signed letters of intent do you have?

- Social Businesses:
    - How many active users do you have daily, weekly, and monthly?
    - How long do users spend engaging with the platform and how do they engage?
    - What does your retention and churn look like?

If The Meeting Goes South

Meetings can go south for a variety of reasons—it can become clear very quickly within 10 minutes of the meeting that the investor is not interested, or that the investor is merely trying to get information out of you that might be helpful to a competitor. Most women and minority founders, myself included, can cite past experiences where investors were unaware they were making sexist or racist statements. In worst case scenarios, investors have made inappropriate advances on founders, and blatant sexist or racist remarks. It might be helpful to get on the same page about definitions:

1. **Discrimination:** the unjust or prejudicial treatment of different categories of people, especially on the grounds of ethnicity, age, sex, or disability.
2. **Sexism:** prejudice, stereotyping, or discrimination, typically against women, on the basis of sex.
3. **Racism:** any prejudice against someone because of their race.
4. **Privilege:** is an advantage or set of advantages that you have that others do not.
5. **Intersectionality:** the belief that our social justice movements must consider all of the intersections of identity, privilege, and oppression that people face.

In the past during uncomfortable conversations with investors, I've really struggled to think through on the spot how best to respond in these high-stakes on-the-spot sensitive situations and definitely made some mistakes along the way. It's hard not to roll your eyes or let your mouth drop to the floor when you hear something so unbelievably discriminatory or inappropriate. It's challenging to experience something like this, immediately pick yourself back up, and not let it affect your demeanor in your next pitch meeting or the rest of the day, mind your mental health in general.

I believe intention matters. If you believe the investor you're talking to *intended* to cause harm or is completely *aware* that what they are saying is discriminatory or inappropriate, it's worth restating what the investor said and ask the person to confirm what they are talking about. If it's clear their intention is bad, then you probably don't want to work with this person and should end the meeting. I think it's best to avoid making stark enemies, even if the person you're interacting with is clearly a bad person. To end the meeting, interrupt the person if needed and say something along the lines of, "Unfortunately something urgent has come up, and I need to end our meeting early. Thanks for your time." and leave.

What if you restate what the investor said and they seem completely unaware that what they are saying is inappropriate (racist, sexist, discriminatory, etc.)? If it's clear they are unaware and don't have negative intent, you have these options of what to do next:

1. Angrily call them out and shame them, and end the meeting. I don't recommend this approach.
2. Decide to attempt to educate the person. This can be a burden on your mental health, and is a gift.
3. Ignore it and move forward with your pitch conversation.
4. Politely say something has come up and you unfortunately need to go, and end the meeting.

During fundraising, you may encounter so many frustrating questions and statements that it may be tempting to call each investor out and tell them explicitly why what they said was wrong, sexist, racist, etc. and then end the meeting. However, if you call someone out—it will likely embarrass them and make them feel shame. According to Santa Clara University Psychology Professor Shauna Shaprio, research shows that shame doesn't help people learn new behaviors and change—shame shuts down the centers of the brain responsible for learning and growth.

I highly recommend avoiding this first approach, because it leaves both parties worse off. It makes the investor feel ashamed and therefore, scientifically shuts their brain down from being able to learn a new way of thinking or new behavior. Your response will also likely make an active enemy out of the investor—and whenever your name or your company name is brought up in conversation, the investor may go out of their way to try and trash you. In my opinion, it's not worth making enemies if you can avoid it. You'll likely make enemies no matter what being a founder and choosing this line of hyper-competitive work, but why make more enemies if you don't have to?

Instead, add what happened during the meeting to your investor notes, and avoid this person and their fund (or funds they may join) in the future. If down the line a founder reaches out to you to ask for advice about investors to work with, you can share the name(s) of investors over the phone with them that you would recommend they avoid.

The second approach puts the onus on you, the person potentially being discriminated against, to use your precious time and mental energy to help educate the other person. How do you educate a person in a way that doesn't make them defensive and shut down? Chris Voss, former lead international kidnapping negotiator for the FBI and author of a popular business book titled *Never Split the Difference* shares a lot of advice that is transferable to navigating these difficult situations. I believe Voss's tactics often produce great results if you want to pursue the gentle education route. Here are four of his tactics:

1. **First, use your voice strategically.** Humans naturally copy the energy of the people they are around. As a result, you can shape the conversation by *how* you deliver a message. Use a positive, engaged-sounding voice to make the listener feel comfortable and encouraged to pay attention to the substance of what you are saying. Refrain from sounding angry and upset, and try to sound like a late-night FM DJ voice: slow, deep, and calm. Using an assertive angry voice will put the listener on the defensive and shut them down.

2. **Second, mirror their language.** The most effective way to help someone think is to force them (unknowingly) to reflect on what they're saying without being condescending and making them feel shame. Don't call out and critique their wrong ideas or harmful language. Instead, repeat back to them the last few words from their sentences. Here is an example conversation:

   Investor: *"I avoid investing in women entrepreneurs that talk openly about being a mom."*

   You: *"Talk openly about being a mom..."*

   Investor: *"Yeah, founders who share on social media that they are a mom and make being a mom part of their personal brand."*

   You: *"Make being a mom part of their personal brand..."*

   Investor: *"Well, every female founder I've seen that's been public about being a mom has gone on to struggle raising future rounds. So I don't invest in women who are open about being a mom."*

This conversation actually happened, and the investor I was speaking to was a new mom herself. I didn't directly call out the discrimination, and instead used a calm, slow late-night FM DJ voice and mirrored the investors' language in order to force her to reflect on what she was saying to me.

I avoided sounding disapproving or angry because my goal wasn't to shame her and make her feel bad—which would have probably caused her to shut down and become closed off to self-reflection and new ways of thinking. My goal is to keep the investor talking and open their eyes to their thinking. As a result, I'm helping them analyze whether they're making good decisions on their own. Coming from a place of kindness and curiosity, instead of shame, gives you the best chance of imparting learning to the investor and perhaps changing their thinking and future behavior. "The attitudes of kindness and curiosity release a cascade of chemicals that turn on the learning centers of our brain, giving us the resources we need for lasting transformation," says Dr. Shapiro.

3. **Third, ask open-ended questions.** The last tactic is to ask genuine questions that get the investor to think about their biases and thought process. Start by asking questions that begin with "how" and make sure to ask open-ended questions, not questions that lead to a "yes" or "no." The goal here is to engage them and draw them into the problem-solving process. It challenges the listener to take responsibility, become aware of a problem, and hopefully find a better alternative for themselves. For example:

You: "*Can you please share some examples of companies you've funded led by founders of color?*"

Investor: "*I fully support founders of color. I don't 'see race'—I see every founder I chat with as equal. I don't know offhand the number of companies in our portfolio founded by people of color, but it's better than the industry average for sure.*"

> ***You:*** *"How have you seen the industry make meaningful progress towards funding more founders of color in general? Curious what things you've tried and see work."*
>
> ***Investor:*** *"I believe the industry has made some progress in recent years towards funding more founders of color, and we work to change this by helping our founders with fundraising, introductions to customers, press, and many more areas. We also go to a ton of industry events hosted by minority founder groups to get dealflow. Are there any you think should be on my radar?"*

Unfortunately, most conversations end up being a mix of good and bad like above. It's extremely problematic for an investor to say they "don't see race"—ignoring race means ignoring long standing problems in the technology industry, our society and history in general, and ignoring important aspects of a person's identity. It also shows a lack of awareness about this serious problem, and it's difficult (if not impossible) to improve a metric like the number of diverse founders you've invested in if you aren't measuring it in the first place.

What's good about this brief conversation is that after being asked open-ended questions, the investor is now reflecting on everything she and her firm does to support and fund founders of color. That's the power of asking an open-ended question that is not tinged with shame or condescension.

You could decide to go with the third option, and ignore whatever inappropriate comment or question the investor says and move forward with your pitch. If what the investor said isn't a deal breaker for you in terms of you still being interested in having the investor onboard, then you don't have to take on the mental load and energy of educating them.

Lastly, if the investor says something that isn't okay with you, you can politely say something like, "I'm sorry—something urgent has come up and I unfortunately need to go right now. Thanks for your time!" and hop off the meeting or leave their office if it's in-person. Choosing whether or not you want to spend the time educating the investor using the tactics shared above is completely up to you and whether or not you feel up to it. Educating people takes your precious time and energy, and is a gift to the other person. You don't owe anyone that gift.

Ideally, you want to work with people who are aware of their privilege and actively working on themselves and within the industry at large to dismantle racism, sexism, and discrimination because it's such a rampant problem.

How To Show Up

When I first arrived in Silicon Valley back in 2016, I had zero clue what the norms were around dress and communication. I showed up to job interviews wearing thrift store-bought stuffy business attire and would address everyone I met via email or in-person formally out of respect as "Ms. Last Name" and "Mr. Last Name." Suffice to say, I wasn't getting any job offers.

After one in-person interview in San Francisco's financial district, a kind woman gave me some feedback after my interview: "You aren't going to get this job or any job in Silicon Valley if you dress and talk like that. You scream 'not a culture fit.' People here dress more relaxed, speak more casually, and use first names when talking to people." My eyes grew wide. I profusely thanked her, and am grateful she gave me that feedback to this day. So many of my interviewers could easily tell I wasn't privy to the culture, and didn't bother giving me this kind of feedback to help me have a better chance of succeeding at my next interview and pursuing a career in Silicon Valley.

Poor Video & Audio Quality = Virtual Meeting Failure

Years later when fundraising, I had the opportunity to pitch Ashton Kutcher, the famous Hollywood actor and founder of Sound Ventures. Kutcher has become a really well-respected VC with great investments in tech companies including Airbnb, Uber, Spotify, and more. I grew up watching Kutcher in shows and movies, and really respected him as an investor.

I was thrilled to have the opportunity to share what I was building with Kutcher and grateful for his time. The pitch occurred over zoom (the industry standard as of this writing for virtual video-call meetings), and I was so excited to see him as we all entered the virtual meeting. My first massive mistake was bringing too many folks from the company into the meeting with me. I was nervous, and thought bringing multiple early team members would show what a great team we were, and help us get to a faster decision.

We all started logging into the zoom meeting. One of my teammates had a unique sense of style, and showed up to this meeting wearing a skintight leopard tube top, large neon hoop earrings, incredibly long heavy-looking fake

The Pitch Conversation

eyelashes, and was loudly smacking chewing gum. After some quick niceties, we launched into our pitch conversation. It became quickly apparent that one of my team member's internet was spotty and their video kept freezing, yet they remained unaware this was happening and kept trying to answer Kutcher's questions.

I watched in horror as Kutcher kept trying to get a word in and let my team member know we could barely hear what they were saying and the connection was bad. As the video kept freezing, my team member started having issues with one of their fake eyelashes falling off, and so they attempted to fix it during the pitch by trying to place it back onto their eye while also loudly chewing gum. Kutcher looked repulsed and horror-struck as the frozen frames showed them trying to replace an eyelash with their mouth wide open and yellow gum mid-chew.

Kutcher finally said, "Enough. Hayley—pick up the pitch." I was completely in shock and mortified. I was so stunned that I couldn't remember my part of the pitch conversation. My mind went completely blank. Kutcher yelled with his hands raised, "Hayley, finish the pitch!!" Looking shell shocked with all of my confidence and excitement completely gone, I uneasily (and probably incomprehensibly) stumbled my way through the rest of the pitch conversation. As you can imagine, we never heard from Sound Ventures again. I'm sure Kutcher will never forget it as one of the most horrible pitches he's ever seen. I still have nightmares about it, but learned never again to bring so many team members into a meeting and also how to set up future virtual meetings for success.

VCs often "pattern match" and do so even more in times of economic recession, because it's seen as safer and more conservative. Pattern matching refers to the practice of using past successes and trends (i.e. choosing to invest in founders who are white, heterosexual, men who look nerdy like Mark Zuckerberg or captivating like Steve Jobs) as a model to guide future investment decisions. Obviously, pattern matching leads to bias by choosing to only invest in founders with certain backgrounds or schools and causes VCs to overlook or pass on founders that don't conform to this pattern.

I've seen startup founders try to copy exactly what their idols have worn—as in wearing black turtlenecks like Steve Jobs which now is synonymous with felon founder Elizabeth Holmes, to millennial pink blazers and outfits which now makes many investors think about the Girlboss-era implosion in the last five years (i.e. The Wing, Girlboss, Glossier, Outdoor Voices, etc.). It's helpful to know what clothing items and colors like these will immediately signal something negative to investors and avoid these.

If you are unsure about what to wear, look up what founders of hot startups in your area are currently wearing and find a similar style. Typically, you can easily check their social media profiles to get a sense for whatever trend is in style.

Having a high quality video and audio call setup not only helps your virtual fundraise meetings be more successful, but it also signals to investors that you are prepared and take your job seriously. It's an easy way to stand out from the pack with the very real benefit of making sure you are prepared in case of a mishap (hello internet outage surprise from hell) and at the very least, having no distracting interruptions that lead to a poor meeting overall.

It's helpful to get a sense for the type of video experience that you believe is high quality. What YouTube creators have you seen that you remember having high quality video? If you can't think of anyone, look up Silicon Valley folks or funds with large YouTube channel followings like Tim Ferris, Garry Tan, Justin Kahn, Andrew Huberman, etc. Check out a few of their videos and note what looks good, and what if anything could be improved. From your favorite YouTubers, Google search their setup. Many YouTubers create videos, blog posts, or post on social everything they use to create their videos. These recommendations can range in price from a few hundred dollars set up to hundreds of thousands of dollars. Below I share some really basic tips for creating a video call setup that will stand out from the pack of other founders raising and also includes a backup plan in case of an unforeseen problem like an internet outage, device not working, etc.

Virtual Meetings and Calls Setup:

- ☐ Ask other founders and investors what video-call tool is the standard in your area. Use this tool.
- ☐ Get the highest quality internet and cell service in your area.
- ☐ Get a computer, laptop, or camera for video calls.
- ☐ Position whatever camera device you are using so that you can look directly into the camera.
- ☐ Get a stable desk or surface (dining room / kitchen table).

- ☐ Get a stand for your phone.
- ☐ Get and always use a ring light. They cost around $20 as of this writing and typically include brightness and temperature controls.
- ☐ Use headphones or a microphone (examples: Apple airpods, yeti microphone, etc.)
- ☐ Make sure your surroundings are as quiet as possible—figure out another location if there is loud construction or other noise distractions in your area that will detract from your pitch.
- ☐ Create a neutral backdrop. The backdrop should not include a bed, open bathroom door, etc. A wall is great, or a bookshelf with plants on top. Alternatively, buy a cheap white backdrop or huge paper board online. Get rid of any clutter, mess, weird or polarizing artwork, and potential distractions.
- ☐ Make sure all of your notifications (computer, phone, watch, etc.) are turned off during the meeting except for emergency contacts (family member, kid's school, babysitter, etc.)
- ☐ DO NOT read from a script. Have your pitch and succinct answers to common questions completely memorized.
- ☐ Have a Plan A & Plan B
    - ☐ Plan A
        - ☐ Use a computer, laptop, or camera and keep it stable on a desk.
        - ☐ Use high quality internet in your area.
    - ☐ Plan B
        - ☐ Use your phone and a phone stand on a desk.
        - ☐ Use high quality cell service in your area.

Chapter 3: The Pitch Conversation
End of Chapter Summary Checklist:

- ☐ The Pitch Conversation:
- ☐ Script for setting up the call for success memorized.
- ☐ Questions for the specific investor.
- ☐ Introduction: Introduce yourself, sharing your background, and why you are the right person to build this company.
- ☐ The Problem: Articulate the problem you are trying to solve, how you encountered it, and how many people have this problem (the market).
- ☐ Your Solution (Service or Product): Share a clear one-liner about what your product is or will be, and then share more about how it works from the user's perspective.
- ☐ Why Now: Why this exact moment in time has unlocked this opportunity. Is there a breakthrough new technology that allows this problem to be solved now, when it hasn't been able to be solved in the past? Is there a major societal shift in behavior or change in government laws?
- ☐ Your fundraising tracks for various parts of your business.

Virtual Meetings and Calls Setup: Have a Plan A & Plan B

- ☐ Plan A
    - ☐ Use a computer, laptop, or camera and keep it stable on a desk.
    - ☐ Use high quality internet in your area.
- ☐ Plan B
    - ☐ Use your phone and a phone stand on a desk.
    - ☐ Use high quality cell service in your area.

Chapter 4

Strategy

As discussed earlier in the book, the fundraising strategy in this book is for pre-product market fit startups, often just a founder or group of co-founders with an idea and without a working product or traction.

Founders will often ask me, "What is a round (pre-seed, seed, Series A, etc.) and how do I know where I fit in? Which round type should I be raising?" The fundraising round name, traction expectations, and amount raised has massively shifted over time. When I raised a seed round for my first company—$4.7 million was considered a massive round for the seed-stage. What you will come to learn when you chat with investors is that all have different expectations for how much traction you should have at the stage you are raising, and many will say you are "too early" instead of just saying "no." Too early is another way of saying no.

Generally speaking, pre-seed is the name of your very first round of financing. It's less common to have a "lead" investor, or an investor that puts in a very large check for a majority of the round. Often people will say part of the round is made up of "friends and family" which means that wealthy family members or friends who are accredited investors invested. As of writing this book, to be an "accredited investor" as defined by the Securities and Exchange Commission (SEC), a person must have an annual income exceeding $200,000 ($300,000 for joint income) for the last two years with the expectation of earning the same or a higher income in the current year.

A person is also considered an accredited investor if they have a net worth exceeding $1 million, either individually or jointly with their spouse. The SEC also considers a person to be an accredited investor if they are a general partner, executive officer, or director for the company that is issuing the unregistered securities. An entity is considered an accredited investor if it is a private business with assets exceeding $5 million. If you are unsure whether or not you, friends, or family members are accredited investors, consult a lawyer. Never take any money from non-accredited investors or it will be a time-consuming mess and difficult down the road.

I had a lot of trouble with this, because it basically bars lower socioeconomic folks from this asset class. Startups like "party round," WeFunder, Angellist and others are working to make this more equitable. Thankfully, there are now more investor-friendly ways to roll up angels into one vehicle, to have a clean cap table, and simplify the signature processes.

Seed and later-stage founders are great to bring onboard at the pre-seed or seed stage, because if they meet the requirements above, they are considered accredited investors by the SEC. They may not have hundreds of thousands or millions of dollars at their disposal yet, but it's worth bringing onboard founders who've raised recently and meet the accredited investor requirement for a few reasons.

Pre-seed rounds are most often made up of a combination of angel investors and pre-seed or seed funds. It's become more common to see "party rounds" for the pre-seed stage, which means a lot of investors making up the total round size. However, it seems most successful startups keep their cap tables 'lean' meaning they don't want too many small checks and investors onboard. This tends to be preferred by later-stage investors.

Pre-seed

- Friends and family
- Less common to have a 'lead'
- Half angels, half funds
- Party round

Seed

- Benefits of having a 'lead'
- Potential downsides of raising from a top-tier fund
- First $1M angels, rest funds and one large check

As we discussed in the timing section, momentum and speed are everything. You don't want to be fundraising forever for many reasons—it's distracting from building your core product and reaching product-market-fit, and it sends a bad signal to the investor community (you'll be perceived as incompetent, as a founder unable to sell, an outsider, etc.). Your goal should be to prepare extremely well, so that you can be as efficient as possible and only be in "fundraising mode" for a short amount of time—maximum a few weeks.

Most investors will say they want to know a founder for a long time before they will write a check. However, at the earliest stages, investors want to get into "hot deals" and typically look down upon founders that spend too much time fundraising. You are on a clock as soon as you start meeting with a VC. If they are interested, they'll ask for frequent coffee meetings or calls. You'll need to demonstrate amazing progress or it'll look bad if you don't provide updates. The more common advice I've seen is to start having these coffee chats and giving updates and building relationships with people about six months from the time you want to raise your Series A round, or when you've started seeing signs of product market fit and are growing month over month.

High-Level Fundraising Strategy:

- Weeks 1-3: Research and outreach
- Week 4: Meetings with venture-backed founders
- Week 5: Meetings with angels & solo capitalists (AKA quick decision makers)
- Third tier → First tier
- Week 6: Third tier funds
- Week 7: Second tier funds
- Week 8: Top tier funds

When you start meeting with venture capital funds, they will likely require 2-3 total meetings to reach a decision. It is absolutely critical that you batch all of those first meetings as close together as you can so that you are able to get decisions from funds around the same time period and maintain momentum during your raise. Here is a breakdown of how you should schedule meetings during a week you are meeting with venture capital funds:

Example Schedule Week 6: Third Tier Funds

Try to schedule every first meeting during the early part of the week on a Monday, Tuesday, or Wednesday (at the latest). Likely, that will mean video calls mostly back-to-back from 6 AM - 8 PM or later. Here is a sample schedule for Monday:

- 5 - 6 AM: Exercise, meditate or do whatever you need to do to get ready and in a great state of mind
- 6 - 6:30 AM: Fund A first meeting

- 6:30 - 7 AM: Fund B first meeting
- 7 - 7:30 AM: Fund C first meeting
- 7:30 - 8 AM: Fund D first meeting
- 8 - 8:30 AM: Fund E first meeting
- 8:30 - 9:30 AM: BREAK. Go to the bathroom, get water, coffee and a snack. Think through the meetings you've had so far and if there are any concerns that are repeatedly popping up. Quickly come up with a better answer to those questions to try for the next batch of meetings.
- 9:30 - 10 AM: Fund F first meeting
- 10 - 10:30 AM: Fund G first meeting
- 10:30 - 11 AM: Fund H first meeting
- 11 - 11:30 AM: Fund I first meeting
- 11:30 AM - 1 PM: BREAK. Repeat everything from the above break, have lunch, and send follow up notes to everyone you've chatted with so far today. For folks who indicated they would be interested in continuing the conversion, schedule more time tonight (6 - 8 PM timeslot below) or early tomorrow morning.
- 1 - 6 PM: Continue 30 minute meeting increments with new funds and take breaks as needed. During breaks, schedule interested folks for the 6 - 8 PM time slot this evening.
- 6 - 8 PM: 30 minute second meetings with VCs you've chatted with today that are very excited and interested.
- 8 - 9 PM: Reflect on how meetings are going, and problem areas. Augment or change parts of your pitch or question answers if the feedback you are receiving is valid.

Weeks 1 - 3: Research and Outreach

By this time, you've completed all of the preparation we discussed in earlier chapters. Now is the time to find names of founders, angels, solo capitalists, funds, and fund partners. Create a spreadsheet or use CRM software to track all of your investor research prep work. You can use my template here, or download it on my website. You'll want to keep tabs on the following:

- Tab 1: Venture-backed Founders
- Tab 2: Angels & Solo Capitalists
- Tab 3: Funds

For each tab, you'll want to track the following in columns:

1. Name
2. Firm Name
3. Title
4. Tier (rank 1st tier, 2nd tier, or 3rd tier)
5. Social Handle
6. Email
7. Status
    - 1 - Outreach Sent X date
    - 2 - Meeting Scheduled
    - 3 - Meeting Completed
    - 4 - Interested
    - 5 - Committed
    - 6 - Invested
    - 7 - Dead
8. Date
9. Lead?
    - Y/N
10. Typical Check Size
11. Ownership requirement?
12. Star Portfolio Co's
13. Favorite Founders
14. Asked for Introductions? (only after signed & wired)
15. Link to Meeting Notes
16. Miscellaneous Notes

Look at the venture capital firm's website in order to learn whether the firm solely leads deals or is willing to participate in rounds. Sometimes firm websites will also share their typical check size. These sites will almost always list portfolio companies, and usually their top-performing companies will be listed first or larger than the rest.

For your target partner at the firm, you need to find out which 'star portfolio companies' are this person's favorite—or in other words, which founders they've invested in that are their favorites, that they really respect and are performing well. If you look at the partner's Twitter, LinkedIn, or other social media profiles, they'll often list their top-performing startups in their bio. An even better way to find out that takes more time, is to research and read their latest blog posts, and podcast interviews. Once you read and listen to a few, you'll hear them repeatedly share examples of founders they admire and respect in their portfolio and you should add those company and founder names to the "start portfolio co's" and "favorite founders" rows in the spreadsheet.

Other ways of finding this information ahead of investor meetings is through the following:

1. **TechCrunch and The Information:** media companies that cover tech and startup companies. Search for the partner's name and favorite founder names within these sites.
2. **Crunchbase:** a platform for finding business information about companies. Often you can find investment funding information, founder names, and news.
3. **AngelList:** a website where you can find funding information about startups, angel investors and their recent deals, and is for job-seekers looking to work at startups. Founded in 2010, it started as an online introduction board for tech startups needing seed funding.
4. **PitchBook:** similar to Crunchbase and Angellist but often more detailed and accurate—a platform that shares venture capital investments in companies.

Meeting Format: Phone Call, Video, Or In-Person?!

It's typical that your first meeting with an angel or venture capitalist will either be over video call (Zoom is the industry standard as of the writing of this book) or phone call. Second and or third meetings with venture capital firms may require you to travel and meet the partner(s) in-person at their office.

For your first meeting, I highly suggest you optimize for a video call over a traditional phone call for a few important reasons. You are selling part of your company, and it's much easier to sell someone that they should work with you and buy into your exciting company over video where you can also convey excitement through your facial expressions, body language, etc.

Some investors might prefer a phone call because they are tired of video calls, want to walk or exercise while talking to you, are driving or at a location bad for video calls like a cafe, or perhaps want to text or do other work while you're talking. In order to have the best chance of success from the founder perspective and ideally have an investor's full attention, opt for a video call over a phone call if you can.

Week 4: Venture-backed Founders

Other founders are your key to a successful fundraise. They are helpful for a variety of reasons ranging from helping you understand what valuation is reasonable, providing off-the-record insights on working with specific investors, helping you seal the deal by advocating for you with their investors, and much more.

How do you get a founder you don't know to respond and talk to you? Similar to investors, show social capital. Do you have any mutual connections? Do they follow anyone you know on Twitter? Look at LinkedIn, Facebook, Instagram, Twitter, etc. You need an online presence and ideally mutual connections. This is why it's helpful to spend time in Silicon Valley before you fundraise and socialize with the right people so when people look you up, they see many mutual connections.

Before a founder or anyone for that matter in the startup ecosystem will respond to outreach or meet with you—they are going to look you up. They will Google your name, search for you on LinkedIn, Twitter, Instagram, etc. We are now living in somewhat of a Black Mirror episode where only the wealthy and uber-successful don't have to maintain their online presence. If you're still trying to make it as a successful founder, or build your reputation as a successful investor, you are working on building your online brand.

Why do investors do this? They want to maintain relevancy and attract the best and brightest founders to seek them out whenever they start fundraising. Why do founders need to do this? For a few reasons:

- First, it strengthens the likelihood that someone will take a call or meet with you by showing you are credible and are not going to ruin a connection if someone opens up their network to you and makes an introduction for you to someone they know.
- Helps in conversations with investors about distribution if you've been able to build an audience of folks that will become future customers.
- Makes it easy for people to tell what you stand for and what your expertise is.
- Having a strong online brand as a founder also increases the likelihood that a journalist will risk their reputation by covering you and what you're building.
- Lastly, building in public is a way of mentoring other aspiring founders at scale.

Understandably, people want mentorship, advice, and access to your network. This should go without saying, but it happens all of the time, including to me—founders will reach out and say: "Can you mentor me?" "Can you review my pitch?" "Can I pick your brain?" "Can you introduce me to X?" "Can you write an article about me?" These first-contact attempts (first time a founder ever hears from you) have close to a zero percent success rate. They never work. As Justin Kan has said, "That's like coming out and saying 'Can we have sex?' as your opening line. That shit doesn't work for the record." Understandably.

Founders have limited time and they are forced to pick and choose who they can help. You should focus on building that relationship, and showing value to the founder before your first reach out.

Week 5: Angels & Solo Capitalists (Quick Decision Makers)

This week is about having as many meetings as possible with quick decision makers—individual investors who will typically invest in you on the spot or after a second meeting. We'll start with a list of accredited investors, and later share some methods for bringing onboard non-accredited investors to your cap table.

As we discussed in an earlier chapter, to be an "accredited investor" as defined by the Securities and Exchange Commission (SEC), you need to fulfill one of the following criteria:

- Earn an annual income exceeding $200,000 ($300,000 for joint income) for the last two years with the expectation of earning the same or a higher income in the current year.
- Have a net worth exceeding $1 million, either individually or jointly with their spouse.
- Be a general partner, executive officer, or director for the company that is issuing the unregistered securities.

If the person does not meet one of these requirements, they are considered a non-accredited investor. As I mentioned earlier, if you are unsure whether or not you, friends, or family members are accredited investors—consult a lawyer. Never take any money from non-accredited investors or it will be a time-consuming mess and difficult down the road.

Here are a few helpful definitions of various investor types:

- **Friends and family:** family, friends, acquaintances, and former coworkers that are accredited investors and want to invest in your startup.
- **Angel investor:** a wealthy individual investing their own capital in startups. Check sizes can range from thousands of dollars to a few million dollars. The "typical" standard check size for angel investors is $25K.
- **Solo capitalist:** a venture fund with only one member on the investment team. This individual is the only person making decisions about the fund and invests check sizes typically ranging from $50K to millions.
- **Party round:** when a funding round consists of many angel investors and/or small checks from funds, with no "lead" or investor with a big stake in the round.

- **Scout:** typically a founder or operator in industry that is able to invest a venture capital fund's money into a startup. Check sizes range from $25K - $50K and the scout typically receives carry.

If you plan on raising "a party round" with many angel investors, the upside is that you won't have an entity with significant control that can affect the outcome of the startup and your job as founder and CEO, along with your co-founders. Folks argue that the downsides include the fact that there are no majority stakeholders in the round—so no one is really incentivized to help you succeed.

Another downside is that if the party round is not set up in a way to keep a clean cap table with a simplified signature process—this could scare away other investors down the road. A stigma still remains in Silicon Valley that founders only raise party rounds because they were unsuccessful in raising from institutional funds. This stigma has lessened over time, but it's worth knowing that it still exists.

It's awesome to see founders have easier and cheaper options available to help lower the barriers of entry to invest in startups. Is there an investor-friendly way to roll up all of your small angel checks into one vehicle, to have a cleaner cap table, and simplify signature processes in the future? In the future and with changing laws, there will hopefully be many more options to simplify and allow non-high-worth family, friends, customers, and more to invest in your company. Raising money from customers specifically can show a tremendous amount of interest and momentum for your company—and can really help you raise money from institutional investors for the rest of your round. We'll talk more about raising from non-accredited investors below.

To bring onboard accredited investors, why would you as a founder want to set up a Roll Up Vehicle [RUV] instead of accepting individual direct investments from angel investors? The main reasons include having a leaner cap table that will be more attractive to future investors and speed. Having fewer names on your cap table is preferable to investors, because it simplifies major company matters down the road. Using an RUV to bring onboard a lot of small checks from accredited investors saves the founder a lot of time, and also simplifies major company matters down the road because each of the investors in an RUV typically doesn't have any voting rights.

Thankfully, there are now more investor-friendly ways to roll up angels into one vehicle, to have a clean cap table, and simplify the signature processes. This is a great option if you are interested in accepting small checks for approximately less than $10,000 from accredited investors including family, friends, strategic angels, customers, users, etc. As of writing this book, the concept of a roll up vehicle [RUV] is fairly new—AngelList just launched their RUV product in 2021. RUVs are special purpose vehicles (SPVs) that make an investment in your company. They provide a way for founders to efficiently allow investors into a round as one entity on a cap table and without expensive legal fees. Similar to SPVs, RUVs are structured as Delaware Limited Partnerships as is typical in venture.

Crowdfunding and Non-Accredited Investors

As we discussed earlier, current regulations bars lower socioeconomic people from the asset class of investing in risky startups. Crowdfunding allows entrepreneurs to raise money from non-accredited investors. Some crowdfunding platforms allow entrepreneurs to sell equity in their company to non-accredited investors or sell products (sometimes before they exist). There is a growing trend wherein founders who care about diversity and inclusion are pursuing crowdfunding for portions of their rounds—typically during seed or Series A.

Examples of startups that have successfully executed on this include Levels, a metabolic health company using WeFunder, and Bobbie, an infant formula company using Republic. For most consumer companies, many of your customers are likely non-accredited investors. Doing a crowdfunding campaign for part or all of a fundraise round allows your customers to get skin in the game, hopefully be rewarded by your continued success, and further incentivizes those people to champion your brand to all of their friends.

To create a crowdfunding campaign, you need to set a duration (typically at least a month) and choose a type of campaign. Some campaigns allow entrepreneurs to sell equity in their startup to non-accredited investors such as the Levels and Bobbie campaigns. Other types of campaigns allow entrepreneurs to seek supporters who pledge funds at various levels to fund new product ideas. Rewards are set at each level of funding, and can vary from receiving a finished product, t-shirt, or perhaps a public thank you.

Furthermore, doing a successful crowdfunding campaign is a strong market validation signal to venture capital funds. A well executed crowdfunding campaign shows that your product is providing real value to people and your customers want to see you succeed. After successful crowdfunding campaigns, Bobbie and Levels went on to raise massive rounds led by top venture capital funds at very high valuations. If you don't yet have a product, it shows people want to buy your idea for a product that doesn't yet exist. An example of a founder who used this strategy is Moiz Ali, founder of Native—one of the fastest-growing deodorant brands in North America. Ali sold units of deodorant before making any actual product. Procter & Gamble acquired Native in 2017 for $100 million.

Examples of platforms that allow non-accredited investors to invest in startups include: Kickstarter, Indiegogo, Republic, WeFunder, and Netcapital. At the time of writing this book, the most popular platforms used by Silicon Valley companies for crowdfunding include WeFunder and Republic. Startups including Zenefits, Chekr, Goldbelly, and Gingko Bioworks have used WeFunder to crowdfund. Startups and VC funds that have used Republic to crowdfund include Gumroad, Backstage Capital, Bobbie, and more. It's important to consult a lawyer before conducting a crowdfunding campaign as there are strict legal regulations and requirements of the company after doing one. What many startups view as a main downside of doing a crowdfunding campaign, is that the law requires you to disclose your financials to the public. If you aren't comfortable disclosing that information, you can't do a crowdfunding campaign.

Week 6: Third Tier Funds

Now we start chatting with funds! As we discussed above, funds typically require 2-3 (potentially more) meetings to reach a decision. This is why it's critical you group as many first meetings as possible towards the beginning of the week, so hopefully you'll get a lot of decisions from funds at the same time or within a few days.

Third tier funds are a list of funds that you don't care about or in other words, you wouldn't be devastated if they didn't want to invest. These funds are purely for you to practice on, understand where you can improve, and quickly iterate on your pitch and answers to questions so that you are in good shape for when you pitch your list of second tier funds.

How do you know whether you should consider a fund third tier? When chatting with venture-backed founders during Week 4, you hopefully got some names of individual VCs or funds that these founders are willing to name as not being helpful, disliked working with, or put their company in a bad spot. You wouldn't want to meet with any VCs that founders mentioned were sexist or racist—avoid those entirely. Third tier funds could be newer funds with partners without great reputations in the industry, or funds that have been around but don't have many well-performing portfolio companies or exits.

Week 7: Second Tier Funds

Second tier funds are investors that you would be satisfied and happy to bring onboard. These investors might not have stellar reputations, but they hold some clout and are respected in the industry. Founders they've worked with may describe them as good to have onboard or be neutral about them. Second tier investors don't have a reputation for being bad to have onboard your cap table or having screwed founders over in the past.

When having pitch conversations with second tier investors, it's worth paying even closer attention to their feedback and patterns of responses to your pitch and iterating as you see fit. These are more sophisticated investors than third tier, and closer to what you'll experience when pitching first tier investors.

Week 8: First Tier Funds

First tier funds are investors you would be thrilled to have onboard, and have an amazing track record as investors in your specific domain or in general. These are folks that other founders highly recommend, said are game-changing, and love working with. Having a first tier fund onboard makes it significantly easier to bring onboard top talent, get customers if you're a B2B business, sell your startup down the line, get press, and help with future financing.

One important caveat to note is that many first tier funds are multi-stage—meaning they invest across stages (pre-seed, seed, growth, etc.). If you bring onboard a first tier multi-stage fund at an early stage like pre-seed or seed, or before you've achieved product market fit, then it can be a death sentence for your startup if that fund doesn't also lead your later rounds. Other potential investors will be spooked if that fund doesn't lead later rounds because it's a bad signal that your startup isn't performing, and can make your startup non-investable by everyone else.

Another important factor to note is that often top tier funds will only invest in one startup they think will "win" a market. Meaning, they will invest in only one startup trying to solve the problem of childcare in the world, and not five different startups all trying to solve the childcare problem using different approaches. This means there is a race for startups working to solve a particular problem to get a specific first tier fund onboard, before they choose a competitor of yours.

What you can offer other founders, angels, solo capitalists and VCs if you think you have nothing (helping from your couch):

I call this method "helping from the couch" because it's that easy—you can build and maintain relationships with people without ever leaving your sofa. This only works however if you are consistent, and help others over a period of time. If you suddenly bombard someone on social media with the method below days before you reach out and ask them for something, you won't come across as genuine and may be perceived as transactional—leaving a bad impression (not what you want).

The method involves carving out a block of time in your schedule once or twice a week to help others and offer value to your existing community or folks you are interested in meeting. Ideally before you reach out to founders asking for their time, they recognize your face or name because you have an online presence, and you've helped amplify their work or helped them with some other "ask" from social media. You can and should continue this method if you have a call or meet with the founder, and hit it off.

Founders typically have social media profiles, and primarily 'live' on Twitter, Instagram, or LinkedIn. Identify which social network the founder you want to reach out to is most active. If for example, the person is most active on Twitter, create a private Twitter list of folks you want to meet and add them. In that block of time you allocated during your week to help people you want to meet, look through recent updates of the person and see if you can either amplify their work, news, or help them with an "ask" they've made.

Often founders will share exciting company news or updates, blog posts, thoughts in the form of a thread. Most folks on the internet are lurkers, and most founders or folks in tech haven't reached Kardashian-level celebrity status with millions of followers constantly sending them messages, commenting, liking, and re-sharing. Most folks in the tech industry look at who likes, comments, and re-shares their content because they look at content creation like a product and want to understand their 'users' or followers that love what they're putting out into the world. That means interacting with these folks on social media can make you stand out and most likely they will remember you.

If you genuinely want to support them and like their work (recent blog post, Tweet thread, photo, etc.), leave a nice comment and share it. That doesn't mean creepily commenting or liking every single post. If the person is a frequent poster, then interacting once or twice a week is enough. After a while of doing this, the founder will recognize your profile and either follow you, or be more likely to open a cold email from you or read a direct message.

It's also common for founders to post "asks"—or public requests for assistance to people who are 'following' them or in their network. Examples of common asks range from, "Hey all! We are hiring entry-level designers at our company. Please DM me if you know of any great candidates!" or "Can anyone recommend any coffee shops in Downtown LA?" or "Any recommendations for great swag vendors for employee gifts?"

Even if you don't know what the best coffee shops in LA are from personal experience, or you haven't worked with swag vendors before—it could save the person some time and you could provide them value by researching those things for 5-10 minutes, and then sending them what you believe to be great recommendations. The person will either follow you and start seeing the content you post, or will at the very least take notice, and remember you. So when you reach out to them asking for 15 minutes of their time in the future, there is a much higher chance this person will reply and be willing to offer their time and also potentially their help.

Etiquette

After you connect with an investor and they agree to a meeting with you, you should promptly (within a few hours ideally) send them a calendar invitation with all of the meeting details and for a meeting length of 30 minutes (unless the investor requests less or more time). In the calendar invite description, provide your full name, LinkedIn, and company name as a helpful reminder to the investor as well as your phone number as a backup in case there are connectivity issues with the video call.

If you are waiting for an investor to join your meeting and you haven't received any emails or texts from them saying they're running late or need to reschedule, then after 5 minutes you should send them a note saying you are in the zoom, excited to chat, and please let me know if you need to reschedule. After 10 minutes of waiting, email the investor and let them know that you haven't heard from them and are going to hop off. Then suggest up to 3 times to meet during your evening 6-8 PM timeslot or very early the next morning. Do not share too much availability or you'll appear desperate and like you are struggling to fundraise. To make people respect your time, you should be respectful of your time as well. If someone blows you off, they should reschedule for a time that works best for you.

For each investor (individual or fund) you speak with, keep a document or spreadsheet handy so you can take quick notes about how they answer your questions, any ideas they provide that could be helpful to you and the business, any competitors they mention, insights they have, articles they mention, and details about themselves they share that you would want to remember (their location, they love kitesurfing, kids names, etc.). Keep these handy and searchable so you can easily tailor follow up notes and refer to this information in future meetings. I highly recommend you keep these documents in google docs, notion, or a spreadsheet as keeping this information in a physical notebook is a nightmare to search through and easily pull up later.

Since you have a packed schedule with so many back-to-back meetings, it's helpful to have your phone nearby with a timer on (not very loud) that lets you know when there are 5 minutes left in your meeting. When the timer goes off, let the investor know that you unfortunately have a hard-stop and need to hop into another meeting in 5 minutes. Then, ask whatever questions you have for them and gauge how excited they are and if they say they are, ask them if they want to chat again this evening (during that 6 - 8 PM or so timeslot). This method also keeps you respectful of everyone's time so you don't make the investor late to their next meeting and so you aren't late to your next meeting. It also has the added benefit of making you look like your time is really in-demand. An investor may try to test you by continuing to talk and seeing if you'll go over in time (i.e. maybe you don't really have another meeting), but it's really important to stay firm and end your meeting so you can get to your next one on time.

Send a follow up email to everyone you chat with by the end of the day (or whatever time you go to sleep). Prioritize sending follow up notes quickly to folks that seem (and ideally vocalized) very interested and try to schedule them for later that day or early the next morning if you can. Refer to your meeting notes and make sure to add personal details to each follow up note.

How to Generate Momentum Before and During Fundraising

There are a few ways of generating momentum before and during fundraising including: continuing to make progress towards your company's key metrics, getting press, and bringing onboard well-respected investors. If you have a product and team, it's critical to continue making progress towards the goals you share with investors and to meet or exceed the goals you share.

I believe many Silicon Valley investors would say that getting press ahead of achieving product market fit is a waste of time, but I believe the contrary. Getting some press right before you fundraise or during your raise can help build the momentum of your raise and also get investors to reach out to you with interest in investing.

Investors are looking to invest in founders that are able to get talent, customers or users, partners, press, and future investors excited about their vision. One way to accomplish this is by getting press to cover your startup. To attract investors and get inbound outreach from them, you should target publications and media outlets that produce content that investors follow. For example, I'd want to try and get coverage by a business publication like *Forbes, Inc, Fast Company, The Information, TechCrunch* or other business-focused publication rather than a niche publication that targets my actual customers or audience like a sector-specific publication. An example of a sector specific publication would be if your startup sells furniture, then targeting a publication like *Dwell, Architectural Digest, Southern Living*, etc. that investors are unlikely to be reading.

This strategy worked well for me when raising a prior pre-seed round. I was able to get a brief mention in a *Forbes* piece, and was flooded with interest from potential investors—some of which weren't on my outreach list. One of those investors ended up investing the largest check into the round and became one of my favorite investors that I've ever worked with.

> "Life is too short to hang out with people who aren't resourceful."

— Jeff Bezos, Founder of Amazon

As a new startup without the credibility of having top investors or celebrity backers onboard, a product, or much of anything—it's unlikely you'll get an entire feature in a publication, but you don't need one. Getting a quote from you or brief mention about what you're building in an article is enough. Similar to creating your investor outreach list, you should create a list of relevant journalists and editors that may care about the problem you are trying to solve and cover your type of company (consumer, B2b, edtech, etc.).

Similar to VCs, journalists live on Twitter. Building your reputation on Twitter for VCs will also help with credibility for reporters. Follow relevant reporters and turn on notifications for them, because they often Tweet opportunities for press coverage. They'll often ask to chat with someone with specific expertise (your expertise) with the hashtag #journorequest and if you as a founder are quick to respond and offer your time, the reporter can end up including your quote, company, or thoughts on a topic.

During your fundraise, as the days and weeks go on you are hopefully bringing onboard more investors. You can share updates with investors you are in conversation with, or about to talk to in order to maintain and build momentum. Below are email templates for outreach and follow ups that show momentum.

Cold Outreach Version 1

Hello Nancy,

I hope you are healthy and doing well! I want to be mindful of whatever you may be experiencing given everything that is going on in the world. If you're open to connecting, I'd love to share the work that we're doing.

My name is Hayley, and I'm the founder of Astrapilot, the world's first AI-powered preschool educator. I'm working to solve a problem I experienced first-hand in the early childhood education space utilizing my expertise in AI and consumer tech. I'm a Forbes 30 Under 30 for consumer tech, YC alum, and previously Co-founded a16z-backed Lunchclub AI—the world's first AI superconnector utilizing LLMs to match millions of young professionals worldwide resulting in jobs, mentorship, friendships, and more.

We officially opened up our pre-seed round last week and ended up being oversubscribed in interest for half the round in 24 hours. We're focused on finding the best partners for the round, and just learned about you and your expertise in edtech. I'd love to find time to chat today or tomorrow if you're interested in what we're building with Astrapilot! I'd be really excited to connect. If now is not a good time, no worries, and please let me know if we can ever be of help.

Warm regards,

Hayley

Cold Outreach Version 2 (Social Capital)

Hello Blake,

I hope you are healthy and doing well! I want to be mindful of whatever you may be experiencing given everything that is going on in the world. If you're open to connecting, I'd love to share the work that we're doing. My name is Hayley, and I'm the founder of Astrapilot, the world's first AI-powered preschool educator. I'm working to solve a problem I experienced firsthand in the early childhood education space utilizing my expertise in AI and consumer tech. I'm a Forbes 30 Under 30 for consumer tech, YC alum, and previously Co-founded a16z-backed Lunchclub AI—the world's first AI superconnector utilizing LLMs to match millions of young professionals worldwide resulting in jobs, mentorship, friendships, and more.

We officially opened up our pre-seed round last week and ended up being oversubscribed in interest for half the round in 24 hours. We're now focused on finding the best partners for the round, and just learned about you and your expertise in consumer from one of our investors, [NAME]. We'd love to find time to chat tomorrow or Tuesday if you're interested in what we're building with Astrapilot! We'd be really excited to connect. If now is not a good time, no worries, and please let us know if we can ever be of help.

Warm regards,

Hayley

Cold Outreach Version 3 (Last Outreach Attempt)

Hi Scott,

I hope you are well and having a great week! Just wanted to follow up one last time with regards to my note above. We ended up officially opening our seed round on Monday and ended up being oversubscribed in interest for the entire round in 24 hours with an offer from a fund to lead the round as well as multiple seed-stage fund offers. On Tuesday, and Wednesday we continued to receive offers to invest.

We're now focused on finding the best partners for the round, and really hoped to connect with you because of your deep expertise in consumer marketplaces. We'd love to find time to chat today or tomorrow if you're interested in what we're building with Astrapilot! We'd be really excited to connect. If now is not a good time, no worries, and please let us know if we can ever be of help.

Warm regards,

Hayley

Cold Outreach Version 4 (Social Media)

Hi Emmersen,

I hope you're having a great week and thanks so much for your reply via Twitter! It's awesome to connect with you. I've included a few highlights about Astrapilot, our timeline, and updates on our round below:

Updates on our round: we officially opened our seed round on Monday and received commitments in interest for over half the round within three days. We've continued to receive offers to invest. We haven't reserved the allocation beyond a few angels that we're really excited about like a [X investor], [Y investor], [Z investor].

We're now focused on finding the best partners for the round and would be really excited to chat with you and the [fund name] team because of your deep expertise in consumer edtech products. We'd love to find time to chat today or tomorrow if Astrapilot sounds exciting to you. We'd be really excited to connect.

Warmly,

Hayley

How to Process and Incorporate Feedback During Your Raise

If an investor passes at such an early stage, pre-product, pre-product market fit, it means you weren't able to convince them that you are the perfect team to attack this problem, that the market is big enough, that you could become a billion dollar company, etc. There could be a whole host of reasons why this is the case—they could have met a competitor that you don't even know about that they're excited about, they could have internal biases they are unaware of that conflicted with your team. Because you're pitching yourself, your team (if you have one), and an idea—when folks decline to invest it can feel like such a personal rejection.

You can and should be asking for their thoughts throughout your pitch conversation, and in a follow up call or email if the investor declines to invest. You should also ask them if they are interested in being kept up-to-date on your progress. Here is an example follow up email after receiving a rejection:

Hi Zack,

Thank you for getting back to me so quickly and during your weekend. I greatly appreciate it!

If you are open to sharing, I'd greatly appreciate your thoughts on what hypotheses you would like to see our team prove and what signals or metrics would make [our company] a compelling business over the next 12-18 months? I realize each company is unique in what makes it a great business, but I'd absolutely appreciate your thoughts here or any other additional feedback. I am always open to all feedback and don't take anything personally.

Thanks again for your time, and I'd love to keep you up-to-date on our progress if you are interested. Please don't hesitate to reach out if I can ever be of help to you or any of your portfolio companies.

Greatly appreciate it,

Hayley

Chapter 4: Strategy End of Chapter Summary Checklist:

High-Level Fundraising Strategy:

- ☐ Weeks 1-3: Research and outreach
- ☐ Create investor CRM
- ☐ Utilize outreach and follow up templates
- ☐ Week 4: Meetings with venture-backed founders
- ☐ Week 5: Meetings with angels & solo capitalists (AKA quick decision makers) Third tier → First tier
- ☐ Week 6: Third tier funds
- ☐ Week 7: Second tier funds
- ☐ Week 8: Top tier funds

Fundraising Strategy CRM Preparation:

- ☐ Research and create a list of 3rd tier, 2nd tier, and top tier funds investors.
- ☐ Research each fund, and choose a partner (a GP).
- ☐ Look at your top tier VC investor partner portfolios, and research (news, social media posts, etc.) and find which portfolio founders are their 'golden childs' i.e. favorites. Make a list of those favorite founders.
- ☐ Look at those founders' early-stage raises, and note which angels invested in those companies.
- ☐ Make a list of angels who've invested in your category (consumer, B2B, CPG, etc.).
- ☐ Create a list of founders, top angels & investors on social media and turn on alerts for those specific people.

- ☐ Carve time blocks out in your calendar 2-3X a week to engage with these people on social media. Reshare podcasts these people are featured in, news articles, reshare their blog posts, etc. with nice and thoughtful comments.
- ☐ Create an online presence. Twitter and LinkedIn matter the most for raising.
- ☐ Make a list of your competitors, and a list of VCs and angels that invested in them. Note that you need to ask if there's a conflict.

"Silicon Valley is a mindset, not a location."

— Reid Hoffman, Co-Founder of LinkedIn and Greylock Capital

Chapter 5

Managing Yourself

Like we chatted about in earlier chapters, fundraising is an ultra-marathon and requires peak performance from the founder. In many American corporate environments today, it is seen as a badge of honor to pull all-nighters, and abandon your personal health in the name of the company. If you are a CEO of a startup, you don't want to live like that. You must treat your mind and body like a professional athlete in order to sustain being a high-performing leader of a high-growth company.

When you plan to undergo the stress of planning for a fundraise is probably the least enticing time to learn how to manage yourself mentally and physically so you can perform your best during the entire process. This chapter includes a wide range of advice from hard lessons learned, what to avoid, and a toolbox of accessible easy tools on how to manage yourself for peak performance.

Why Managing Yourself Matters

While you are fundraising, investors are assessing you to determine whether or not you quite literally appear to be a high-performing individual in the CEO/founding role, attractive leader for talent, future investment, and press, be a great steward of capital, and in my opinion most importantly—that you understand and take seriously that you are responsible for your employees *livelihoods*. If you physically appear like you are unable to take basic care of yourself, how are you going to survive the long-haul incredibly challenging journey of creating a multi-billion dollar company?

Every day as a startup CEO presents incredible highs and lows, and investors are evaluating whether or not you have what it takes for this extremely demanding long-term job. How you carry yourself, whether you look exhausted, what you are wearing, how you speak—all of these things are being assessed by investors to determine whether or not they think you will succeed.

The old adage from the airline industry "put your own oxygen mask on before helping others" is extremely important in high-stress professions like being a founder. This metaphor emphasizes the importance of taking care of your well-being first, so you can show up and perform your best at your job. I hate the term "self-care" which sounds so narcissistic and vain to me. Prioritizing and taking care of your health mentally, emotionally, and physically so you can be a more effective leader is not a selfish act. It's critically important. You cannot show up and perform your best as a startup founder or in your personal life as perhaps a parent, partner, or family member if you are not in good condition yourself.

The advice in this chapter is about what you can control to set yourself up for the best chances of success. We cannot change people's aware or unaware biases and prejudices against women and minority founders. By better understanding the norms and way this industry works in terms of evaluating founders, I hope this section provides you with helpful advice to feel and perform better in your everyday job as a startup founder and while fundraising, and share my mistakes so hopefully you can avoid them along your journey.

An unfortunate truth about the difficult startup founder job is that entrepreneurs are far more likely than the general population to experience mental health issues. A 2015 UC Berkeley study titled, "Are Entrepreneurs 'Touched with Fire?'" investigated the prevalence and characteristics of mental health conditions among founders. Among 242 entrepreneurs and demographically matched comparison participants studied, the researchers found that self-reported mental health concerns were present across 72% of the entrepreneurs in the sample, which was significantly higher than the comparison participants.

The entrepreneurs were also significantly more likely to report a lifetime history of depression (30%), ADHD (29%), substance use conditions (12%), and bipolar diagnosis (11%) than were comparison participants.

Furthermore, a fact that may not be surprising to folks who've worked in startups before—CEO is the number one career choice for psychopaths according to Kevin Dutton, a British psychologist and writer who specializes in the study of psychopathy. According to *Psychology Today*, psychopathy is a spectrum disorder and psychopaths feature traits such as lack of empathy, pathological lying, and impulsivity. *Psychology Today* editors cite multiple studies displaying that psychopaths exist across cultures and ethnic groups, and it's estimated that approximately 1 percent of males and 0.3-0.7 percent of females globally could be classified as psychopaths.

That number is very different in corporate leadership. In a 2021 *FORTUNE* article titled "12% Of Corporate Leaders Are Psychopaths. It's Time To Take This Problem Seriously," the author and University of San Diego School of Business professor Simon Croom shares that psychopaths are far more prevalent among leadership positions. "Psychopaths are far more prevalent in corporate management than in the general population—about 3.5 to 12 times more according to estimates. And they may be even more common in the top office, with one analysis finding that one in five CEOs could be a psychopath," states Simon.

In his book, *The Wisdom of Psychopaths: What Saints, Spies, and Serial Killers Can Teach Us About Success*, Dutton argues that you are likely to find a lot of functional psychopaths in the CEO role because of their ruthlessness, charismatic personalities, fearlessness, and ability to make quick decisions.

Practice Good Hygiene to Avoid Getting Sick

Before and during fundraising you should be doing everything within your power to avoid getting a cold, the flu, or other sickness that would make you appear incapacitated during fundraise meetings. A lot of the advice I share in this chapter from exercise to nutrition includes habits and tools that support a strong immune system. You may have this advice tattooed in your brain by now because of how often it was repeated during the pandemic. If so, I hope these tips serve as a gentle reminder. Here are some other helpful tips to reduce your exposure to pathogens during this critical time:

1. **Get vaccinated.** Make sure your vaccinations are up-to-date, including the flu vaccine and whatever other vaccines are recommended by your doctor.

2. **Wash your hands and use hand sanitizer.** Use soap and water and scrub for at least 20 seconds. Use hand sanitizer with a minimum of 60+ percent alcohol. Keep your hand sanitizer in your pocket or bag and use it religiously after touching public ATMs, self-checkouts, etc. cesspools of disgusting bacteria.

3. **Avoid sick people.** You probably don't have time anyway to hangout with friends or date, but now is especially a good time to avoid people in-person if you can to prevent yourself from getting sick. You will be meeting a lot of new investors in-person as it is. If you need to meet with someone outside of your fundraising efforts,

ask them beforehand if they have any symptoms or were exposed to anyone sick recently.

4. **Wear a mask.** If you need to go to a grocery store or another potentially crowded indoor place, time to dust off or buy a new N95 mask. If you are unfortunately fundraising during a wildfire situation, avoid going outside and wear an N95 or P100 respirator mask.

Avoid Illegal Substances and Alcohol

There is a lot of advice in Silicon Valley that carries more potentially dangerous implications for founders and employees. In a 2023 *Wall Street Journal* article titled "Magic Mushrooms. LSD. Ketamine. The Drugs That Power Silicon Valley," journalists Kirsten Grind and Katherine Bindley state that "entrepreneurs including Elon Musk and Sergey Brin are part of a drug movement that proponents hope will expand minds, enhance lives and produce business breakthroughs." This and many other articles have asserted that Silicon Valley startup culture sees drugs like psychedelics as alternatives to antidepressants, gateways to unparalleled creativity, and business breakthroughs.

Many psychedelics are still illegal in most places and are considered dangerous because of their unpredictable effects, potential for triggering serious or lasting mental health issues for individuals with prior mental health issues, impairing judgment, harmful misuse, legal risk, and more. While Silicon Valley culture may be full of folks using these substances, I recommend being extremely skeptical, cautious, and weighing the risk/reward in partaking for yourself. It's absolutely possible to achieve peak performance and be creative without the aid of illegal substances and other drugs, and perhaps in a more sustainable, long-term healthy way. I strongly suggest avoiding these substances and alcohol in general, but especially while fundraising.

Why alcohol? Isn't it completely legal, ubiquitous, and dates back eight thousand years? Just because it's legal, doesn't mean it's safe. In recent years, more and more evidence is making it clear that any amount of alcohol is detrimental to your health. Alcohol metabolizes into a chemical that is toxic to your cells and damages your DNA. The consumption of alcohol undermines every single thing you do to preserve your health and youth. If your top priorities include your company and maintaining your health as best you can to perform your best and avoid disease, then cutting out alcohol entirely is a no-brainer.

Big alcohol is a $1.5 trillion industry, made up almost entirely of sixteen companies (all run by men), and alcohol kills over 3 million people a year globally. What most people believe to be true of alcohol today is exactly what Americans believed to be true of cigarette smoking in the early 20th century—that it is a digestive, an appetite suppressant, or an antidote to anxiousness and not bad for you in moderation. If you are interested in learning more, I highly recommend listening to Stanford Professor Andrew Huberman's podcast episode titled "What Alcohol Does to Your Body, Brain & Health" and reading New York Times bestselling book by Holly Whitaker, "Quit Like A Woman: The Radical Choice To Not Drink In A Culture Obsessed With Alcohol." It's easy in our society to drink and much harder, and more contrarian not to imbibe.

Your Toolbox

If you were to ask VC or angel investors for advice or hacks on how to perform your best—you'll likely receive a lot of recommendations that are inaccessible cost-wise to most early-stage founders (and most of society in general). These wealthy folks might recommend you get yourself an $3,995 Eight Sleep mattress and pod to help your "sleep fitness" or buy the $7,500 The Plunge cold plunge tub to help you recover better from working out and elevate your energy levels.

Matt Mochary, dubbed the Silicon Valley CEO Coach and author of the popular book, *The Great CEO Within*, shares his advice for "Parenting As A CEO" in an article on his website mocharymethod.com. He advises that CEOs delegate parts of parenting that "don't energize you" and recommends that you hire the following roles:

1. 1 full-time night nurse
2. 1 full-time daytime nanny
3. 1 weekend nanny to give time off to the full-time night nurse and daytime nanny
4. 1 full-time personal Chief of Staff

Mochary goes on to share that the market in the United States for a top-tier night nurse in 2021 was $200,000 a year. "Be willing to pay it," Mochary advises. Similar to the sticker shock above, this advice is certainly inaccessible to most people at the beginning of their company building journey. Below I share tactical, easy-to-follow, accessible to everyone, and affordable tools you can add to your rotation.

Nutrition

Founder friends of mine over the years shared interesting "hacks" around meals and nutrition that allow them to spend as little time as possible thinking about, planning for and preparing, and eating food. I've witnessed founder friends only consuming meal replacement drinks like Soylent or Ample to get through fundraising periods so they don't have to spend any time thinking about food. I've even had a friend share that during fundraising she would eat baby food pouches whenever she felt hungry. While these tips might work in the short-term for some people, I believe these hacks are unsustainable long-term.

I highly recommend to anyone that you see a primary healthcare M.D. and perhaps a dietitian to get a blood panel done to understand your current nutritional health, what foods you should add or avoid to better your health, and any problems that may need addressing with medical care.

I'm not a nutritionist, but prior to becoming a startup founder I trained as a chef at Le Cordon Bleu, a rigorous and prestigious culinary school and one of the oldest culinary schools in the world. What you eat you literally become, and quality food is critical for fueling not only your body, but also your mind. I try to eat as healthy as possible so I can perform my best and avoid disease, and I believe my food philosophy is pretty universal and can be easily followed:

- **Avoid highly processed foods.** Emerging research suggests a potential link between highly processed diets and mental health issues, including depression and anxiety, and increased risk of obesity and cancer. Highly processed foods are recognizable because they often have a nutrition label and in many grocery stores they are found in the aisles in the middle of the store. Generally speaking, you want to buy food products with few ingredients that you can recognize and pronounce. Many processed foods are high in added sugars, unhealthy fats, sodium, low in nutrients, and potentially contain harmful additives, preservatives, and artificial colors.
- **Eat organic, free-range vegetables and meat whenever possible.** Eating organic foods is better for your health, the environment, and is more ethical. Organic farming practices avoid the use of harmful

synthetic chemicals including pesticides and herbicides. Organic meat and dairy products come from animals that are not given antibiotics or synthetic hormones. These animals are generally raised under conditions that meet basic animal welfare standards and typically have access to outdoor space.

- **Eat the rainbow.** Aim to incorporate a variety of colors and types of foods, spices, etc. to ensure a diverse range of essential vitamins and minerals.

- **Eat fermented foods rich in probiotics.** These foods are associated with increasing gut health, support your immune system, and reduce inflammation. A healthy gut microbiota is also associated with positive effects on mental health, including reduced symptoms of anxiety and depression. Examples of fermented foods rich in probiotics include yogurt, kefir, sauerkraut, kimchi, miso, tempeh, fermented pickles, etc.

"Eat food. Not too much. Mostly plants."

— Michael Pollan, Author and UC Berkeley Journalism Professor

While fundraising, you will be talking *a lot*. Unless you are an actor, you are probably going to talk more during a single day of fundraising than ever before. I believe it's essential to take steps to prevent vocal strain and maintain your vocal health so you appear healthy during your raise and not like you're sick or a chainsmoker. Here are some strategies to prevent a sore throat and raspy voice:

1. **Stay hydrated.** More on hydration below, but it's helpful to avoid diuretics like too much caffeine and alcohol entirely which are dehydrating.
2. **Give your voice periods of rest.** Whatever small amount of time you have outside of fundraising is a great time to give your vocal cords a break and allow them to recover.
3. **Get a humidifier.** You can use a humidifier (they cost around $20 and upwards) in your bedroom while you are sleeping and throughout the day to add moisture to dry indoor air. It's especially helpful during dry winter months. This is a hack that professional singers use in order to maintain their vocal cords for concert tours.
4. **Soothe your throat as prevention.** In the morning, between meetings, and at night drink warm beverages to soothe your throat.

Hydration

The amount of water a person needs to drink is highly individual—it depends on various factors including age, sex, weight, physical activity level, whether you are pregnant, etc. Consult a medical doctor or registered dietitian who can advise you on your individual needs.

Once you know the amount of water you should be drinking a day, a tool I've found to be extremely helpful in setting myself up for success so I almost never need to think about drinking water or be interrupted to get more water is by purchasing a "daily water intake bottle" or sometimes interchangeably called a hydration tracker bottle. This type of water bottle is designed to help people easily meet their daily water intake goals and has markings to provide a visual guide of how much water you should drink by what time in the day to stay hydrated. They come in a variety of sizes so you can find one that meets your personal needs, and they also sometimes include fun encouraging phrases with each time mark like "good morning!" or "you've almost made it!"

These bottles are also reusable and portable which is great for bringing with you while hopping from fundraising meetings. Look for a bottle made from durable materials such as stainless steel, glass, or BPA-free plastic and with features making it easy to carry, such as having a handle or a loop. This kind of bottle can be easily purchased online and ranges in price from $8 - $25+.

Music

Something simple I've found that helps me get into a more confident state of mind, overcome anxiety, fear, and even an extreme phobia is music. Whenever I felt a wave of anxiety and fear—from preparing for a fundraising meeting or literally while I was physically about to enter a meeting—specific music helps me calm down, refocus, and breathes confidence back into my body so that I carry myself with confidence.

Just Watch Me Playlist:

- Never Give Up - Sia
- Dreams - Gryffin
- The Man - Taylor Swift
- The Greatest - Sia
- Titanium (feat. Sia) - David Guetta

Power Posing

There is some really interesting science at play here proving that the mind follows the body. When you smile more, you start to actually feel *happier* over time. When you intentionally carry yourself with confidence you may eventually start to feel more confident mentally.

One of the most viewed TED Talks of all time with over 69+ million views is "Your Body Language May Shape Who You Are" by American social psychologist Amy Cuddy. In her talk, Cuddy asserts that body language affects how others see us, and also changes how we see ourselves. She argues that "power posing" or standing in a posture of confidence where you are standing straight with your feet firmly on the ground hip-distance, with your hands on your hips like a superhero, even when you don't feel confident, can boost feelings of confidence and impact your chance of success before an endeavor.

Sleep Hygiene Tips

Maintaining consistent, high quality sleep so you can focus, stay alert, and perform during the day is absolutely key. It's also very important for overall physical and mental health. A great way to achieve this is by prioritizing sleep hygiene—a few habits that are necessary and work for you to get a good night's rest. Here are a few simple and inexpensive ideas for habits that can improve your sleep hygiene and enhance your productivity and stamina during the day:

1. **Cool bedroom temperature.** Generally a slightly cool bedroom temperature around 60 to 67 degrees Fahrenheit (15.6 to 19.4 degrees Celsius) is recommended for most adults. Studies have shown that cooler temperatures can lead to more restful sleep with fewer awakenings throughout the night and also promote increased proportions of REM sleep, a critical stage of the sleep cycle associated with dreaming and memory processing. Use breathable bedding, light pajamas, and even using fans or other cooling devices can help maintain a cooler sleep temperature.

2. **Blackout sleeping room.** Studies have also shown that sleeping in a blackout or darkened environment offers several benefits rooted in our biology and sleep physiology from circadian rhythm regulation to increasing REM sleep. You can find inexpensive blackout sleep masks online or likely at your local drug store. I personally love Manta Sleep Masks which are extremely comfy, protect your eyelashes, and cost around $25+.

3. **Consistent sleep schedule.** As often as you can, go to bed and wake up at the same time every day, even on weekends. Consistency reinforces your body's natural sleep-wake cycle.

4. **Limit screen exposure before bed.** This is perhaps the most difficult tip when you are fundraising and working long hours with your face glued to your laptop. The blue light emitted by phones, computers, and TVs can unfortunately interfere with your body's production of the sleep hormone melatonin. If you can, try to avoid blue light for at least an hour before bedtime and instead engage in a calming activity like reading a book, meditating, restorative yoga, stretching, journaling, or other soothing signals to your body that it's time to wind

down. You can also wear a pair of blue light glasses to block out blue waves if you need to continue using screens until bedtime.

5. **Avoid or limit caffeine and alcohol.** Both caffeine and alcohol can interfere with sleep. Caffeine can stay in your system for hours, and blocks adenosine—a neurotransmitter that promotes sleep and relaxation. Too much caffeine can also raise your cortisol levels. Caffeine can be present in tea, chocolate, energy bars, etc. Stanford-trained physician and longevity medicine expert Peter Attia, MD, shares in his popular podcast *The Drive* that drinking alcohol is like getting hit unconscious with a baseball bat—you may appear to fall asleep quickly and look like you're asleep, but you are not getting high quality sleep.

If you constantly struggle with sleep and feel exhausted all of the time even when you aren't fundraising, it might be time to consult with a sleep specialist and get a sleep study or sleep apnea test ordered by your doctor. The relevant medical professional can identify any underlying issues you may have, such as sleep disorders, that might be affecting your sleep quality.

"I learned that focus is key, not just in running a company, but in your personal life as well."

— Tim Cook, CEO of Apple

Exercise

Preparing and executing on a fundraise is an extremely difficult time to fit in exercise and not an ideal time to start a new complicated exercise training regimen. However, exercise provides so many short and long-term benefits for both your mind and body, it's worth trying to fit it in if you can. Here's a breakdown of the mental and physical advantages of physical activity and why it's so beneficial:

Mental Benefits Of Exercise:

1. Mood Enhancement: Exercise releases endorphins, which are natural mood lifters. It can help reduce feelings of depression, anxiety, and stress.
2. Improved Cognitive Function: Regular physical activity can boost memory and cognitive function due to increased blood flow to the brain.
3. Stress Reduction: Exercise can help lower the body's stress hormones, such as cortisol, and stimulate the production of endorphins, which act as natural painkillers and mood elevators.
4. Better Sleep: Physical activity can promote better sleep, aiding in falling asleep faster and deepening sleep.
5. Increased Self-Esteem and Confidence: Meeting exercise goals and improving physical appearance can boost one's self-worth.
6. Mindfulness and Meditation: Activities like yoga and tai chi also incorporate elements of meditation and can increase mindfulness.
7. Enhanced Creativity: Some people find they are more creative after a workout.

Physical Benefits Of Exercise:

1. Weight Management: Exercise increases the metabolic rate, helping burn more calories and assisting with weight loss or maintenance.
2. Strengthening Muscles and Bones: Weight-bearing and resistance exercises can increase bone density and muscle mass, reducing the risk of osteoporosis and sarcopenia.

3. Increased Energy: Regular physical activity can boost endurance and help the cardiovascular system work more efficiently.
4. Reduced Risk of Chronic Diseases: Exercise improves insulin sensitivity, cardiovascular fitness, and body composition while reducing blood pressure and blood fat levels. This can help prevent conditions like type 2 diabetes, heart disease, and stroke.
5. Improved Cardiovascular Health: Exercise strengthens the heart and improves circulation, reducing the risk of cardiovascular diseases.
6. Enhanced Lung Capacity: Aerobic exercise can increase lung capacity and overall lung health.
7. Better Skin Health: Increased blood flow from exercise can help nourish skin cells and keep them healthy.
8. Improved Digestion: Regular physical activity can help regulate digestion and prevent constipation.
9. Pain Reduction: Exercise can help reduce pain and improve mobility in people with osteoarthritis. It's also been shown to help with chronic pain management.
10. Longevity: Regular physical activity is associated with a reduced risk of premature death.
11. Enhanced Immune Function: Moderate, regular exercise can boost the immune system, although excessive or intense exercise without adequate rest can suppress it.
12. Flexibility and Mobility: Exercises like stretching or yoga improve flexibility and overall mobility, reducing the risk of injuries.

It's always advisable to consult with a healthcare professional to devise an exercise plan tailored to your individual ability, health needs, and goals. I find it's helpful to understand what's normal for most Americans and comparatively, what's normal for Silicon Valley folks. According to the U.S. Bureau of Labor Statistics' American Time Use survey, the average American's workout routine for men is an average of 2 hours and 18 minutes per week; for women, it's roughly 1 hour and 45 minutes.

In 2023, *The Information* polled over 500 Silicon Valley folks in a first ever "Brain-Body Investment Survey" inquiring about their exercise and wellness habits. "Tech leaders work out twice as much as the average American adult—

and spend 10 times more to do it," according to *The Information* journalist Annie Goldsmith. The majority of survey respondents reported spending five to 10 hours per week exercising, though 12% said they spend over 10 hours a week working out. Across respondents, the most popular fitness routines included weightlifting and strength training, running, and spinning.

So what is the bare minimum amount of exercise you should be getting in general and especially during this extremely busy time? Three hours a week total is a great goal for busy people who want to achieve the greatest gains in benefits. The Stanford-trained physician and longevity expert I mentioned earlier Dr. Attia says, "Going from no exercise to three hours a week approximately reduces your all cause mortality, that is to say death by every cause, by 50% at any moment in time. You're much better off trying to do 30 minutes of exercise six times a week than three hours once a day." He further shares that low intensity cardio for someone that's not physically fit amounts to brisk walking where you feel out of breath enough that you can barely carry out a conversation.

While three hours a week of exercise is my personal goal thanks to Dr. Attia's recommendation, I unfortunately don't always achieve it as a startup founder during especially busy periods like fundraising. The Apple Watch is the best device I've found (and I've tried many) to track exercise and how my VO2 max, a common metric for assessing cardiovascular fitness and aerobic endurance capacity, is improving over time.

An easy hack to get some movement into your day is by taking every meeting or call outside of fundraising, as a movement meeting. For in-person meetings, instead of meeting for coffee and sitting at a cafe—ask if the person you're meeting with is up for a coffee walk. Movement such as brisk walking, biking on a stationary bike, or stepper while on phone calls with co-founders, teammates, friends, and family is a great way to get more out of your time and easily get some movement in your busy schedule.

"Exercise is by far the most potent longevity 'drug.' No other intervention does nearly as much to prolong our lifespan and preserve our cognitive function."

— Peter Attia, MD, Author of
Outlive: The Art & Science of Longevity

Chapter 6

Common Mistakes

Fundraising is one of Silicon Valley's best-kept secrets. It's notoriously difficult to raise venture capital, and even more challenging if you don't have contacts in the ecosystem who've successfully raised before that you can tap for advice. When I fundraised for the first time, I chatted with more than a hundred extremely kind founders who answered my cold messages, offering me helpful advice. Below I share some of the advice I found helpful and mistakes I made during my fundraising journey:

Beware Of Scouts And Conflicts Of Interest

When fundraising for the first time, I met a seemingly nice successful founder with a really impressive background. He previously sold his startup for a lot of money, had a Harvard MBA, formerly worked at Google, etc. The man reached out to me and said he was a huge fan of what I was building, and wanted to meet for coffee. We met, and he asked me a lot of questions about my startup, my pitch, and the dream investors I wanted to work with.

As I started fundraising, I learned that this former founder reached out to some of the dream investors I mentioned to him and pitched my startup without my permission. These investors said they weren't interested and passed on the deal. I never got the opportunity to chat with them myself.

This former founder was trying to curry favor with these investors by surfacing what he thought was a great deal to them, but he never asked me for permission and all of those investors he reached out to passed--closing those doors for me. No one can pitch your startup as well as you can, and make sure you avoid folks like this former founder who may try to go out and pitch on your behalf to ingratiate themselves with investors in hopes of scout or job positions at venture firms.

Accepting Introductions From Non-committed Investors

Never take introductions from investors that have not "committed" to your round. Some folks in the industry define "committed" as getting a handshake deal from an investor where they verbally agree to invest. I define an investor being "committed" as an investor that has signed the necessary paperwork and has wired funds to your company bank account.

In the past, I've had multiple handshake deals with investors where they verbally commit to investing, and then they don't follow through with signing the paperwork and wiring the investment. I've also had investors sign the paperwork and never wire the money. Some of those folks made introductions for me to other investors, and all of those introductions never panned out, likely because these investors found out that the investor that introduced me backed out.

If an investor introduces you to another, and they back out, that is an extremely bad signal. Both of those investors are likely to discuss why the investor backed out after committing verbally to invest. As a founder, you also don't want to ask investors who haven't committed at all to make an introduction for you to another investor. The same conversation will occur where the investor you were introduced to asks the other why they haven't invested, and that's a bad signal.

To avoid awkward and bad situations like those described above, you should only accept introduction offers, or ask for introductions, once an investor has fully committed to your round by signing and wiring.

Don't Skip Due Diligence On Investors

If your company is successful, you'll likely be working with early investors you bring onboard for more than a decade--much longer than the length of an average marriage in the United States. Bringing onboard a bad partner can potentially be devastating for your company down the road. Conducting due diligence on angels and venture firms that write large checks is critical.

I recommend using the angel or venture capitalist's website, Crunchbase, Pitchbook, and news sites like *TechCrunch* to find companies in their portfolio that the investor would define as a "failure." A "failed" founder is one whose company had an outcome that was not what their investor wanted--the company dissolved, sold for a small amount of money, or had a recent down round. Research companies in the investor's portfolio in the news, and find which meet any of those criteria and reach out to those founders.

When reaching out to those founders, keep the message short and ask if they have a quick five minutes of time to chat about their experience working with the investor you're considering working with, include your phone number, and say you can chat any time that's most convenient for them. When they call you, promise to keep the conversation completely confidential and brief, thank them profusely for taking the time, and offer to help them in any way. Ask them:

1. What was your experience like working with the investor or firm?
2. Did you raise money from them again for your next company, or would you fundraise from them again if you started another company? If they are willing to share, why or why not?
3. When times were tough for your startup, what was this investor like?
4. Would you recommend other founders work with them?

"As a startup CEO,
I slept like a baby.
I woke up every
two hours and cried."

– Ben Horowitz,
Co-Founder of Andreessen Horowitz

Chapter 7

Conclusion

Entrepreneurship is a difficult and lonely career path with so much tactical how-to-actually-get-it-done knowledge network and referral bound to few. This book is my attempt to demystify and codify one of the most complicated and unintuitive processes I've learned to do in my career. I sincerely hope it offers you value, paving a more transparent and expedited path for your company to succeed.

The world urgently needs more women and minority venture-backed founders tackling our most pressing global challenges. Ensuring women and minority founders have the opportunity to raise venture capital for their businesses will allow for more varied perspectives and innovative solutions, paramount to harnessing the full spectrum of human potential to address these challenges. Societal values are changing and recognize there is massive untapped potential within diverse entrepreneurial ecosystems. Humanity and our planet today face a myriad of complex problems. We need more brilliant founders like yourself working to solve these problems.

Your time is finite, and life is so short. My ask is that you spend your valuable time as an entrepreneur working towards solving meaningful problems that will better humanity and our planet. The world doesn't need more Juicero-like products, or startups building for the ultra-affluent. If you are looking for problems to work on, or back to the drawing board with your startup—below is a list of the United Nations Sustainable Development Goals (SDGs) which are a list of goals designed to address a wide range of global problems.

The United Nations Sustainable Development Goals:

1. **No Poverty:** End poverty in all its forms everywhere.
2. **Zero Hunger:** End hunger, achieve food security and improved nutrition, and promote sustainable agriculture.
3. **Good Health and Well-being:** Ensure healthy lives and promote well-being for all at all ages.

4. **Quality Education:** Ensure inclusive and equitable quality education and promote lifelong learning opportunities for all.
5. **Gender Equality:** Achieve gender equality and empower all women and girls.
6. **Clean Water and Sanitation:** Ensure availability and sustainable management of water and sanitation for all.
7. **Affordable and Clean Energy:** Ensure access to affordable, reliable, sustainable, and modern energy for all.
8. **Decent Work and Economic Growth:** Promote sustained, inclusive, and sustainable economic growth, full and productive employment, and decent work for all.
9. **Industry, Innovation, and Infrastructure:** Build resilient infrastructure, promote inclusive and sustainable industrialization, and foster innovation.
10. **Reduced Inequality:** Reduce inequality within and among countries.
11. **Sustainable Cities and Communities:** Make cities and human settlements inclusive, safe, resilient, and sustainable.
12. **Responsible Consumption and Production:** Ensure sustainable consumption and production patterns.
13. **Climate Action:** Take urgent action to combat climate change and its impacts.
14. **Life Below Water:** Conserve and sustainably use the oceans, seas, and marine resources for sustainable development.
15. **Life on Land:** Protect, restore, and promote sustainable use of terrestrial ecosystems, manage forests sustainably, combat desertification, halt and reverse land degradation, and halt biodiversity loss.
16. **Peace, Justice, and Strong Institutions:** Promote peaceful and inclusive societies for sustainable development, provide access to justice for all, and build effective, accountable, and inclusive institutions at all levels.
17. **Partnerships for the Goals:** Strengthen the means of implementation and revitalize the global partnership for sustainable development.

"Conventional corporations are at the center of the ring, and eventually they will die off, through either their own misdeeds or catastrophic events, such as dismal economic climates or unforeseen competition. Only those businesses operating with a sense of urgency, dancing on the fringe, constantly evolving, open to diversity and new ways of doing things, are going to be here one hundred years from now."

– Yvon Chouinard, Founder of Patagonia and Environmentalist

Along your entrepreneurial journey and beyond, my other ask is that you do everything within your power to support and champion other women and minority-founded companies at every opportunity along the way. I believe it's a moral imperative and possible no matter how busy you are, or how much money you have. Here are some ways you can pay it forward and create a more diverse and inclusive startup ecosystem:

Lifting Others As You Rise: How To Pay It Forward

Angel Invest

If you are privileged enough to become a venture-backed founder, you are likely now considered an accredited investor by the SEC. If so, please consider supporting startups by investing directly or participating in RUVs. If you aren't an accredited investor, you can support startups through crowdfunding campaigns and platforms specifically for non-accredited investors.

You can be upfront and transparent with founders that you are busy building your company and that all you can contribute is a small amount of capital and not your time. You don't need to become an involved angel investor—spending a lot of time doing due diligence on startups or sourcing dealflow. Many founders will eventually approach you and ask if you would like to get involved in what they are building. Your monetary support, even if it's a very small check of a hundred dollars, can make all the difference for another founder.

Mentorship & Grant Programs

When your startup is able, you can pay it forward by providing grants and mentorship programs to fledgling diverse startups in your space. For example, makeup and skincare startup Glossier provides small grants to diverse startup founders building companies in the beauty space. Crown Affair, a direct-to-consumer haircare brand, provides up-and-coming talent interested in the haircare industry a wonderful mentorship matching program and learning opportunities. These are great ways to build good will for your brand, attract top talent, and do good.

Advocate & Elevate Others When They Aren't in the Room

Accolades like Forbes 30 Under 30, Inc Female Founders 100, and many more signal credibility to investors, potential employees, and the press. When the opportunity arises to nominate folks, dedicate a short amount of time to submit nominations for diverse founders for these opportunities. If you see journalists and editors asking for founder recommendations for a story on social media, similarly advocate they interview or invite on air diverse founders.

Virtual Office Hours

It may be impossible to respond and agree to have a 1:1 call to every aspiring founder that reaches out to you asking for advice. Thankfully, there are more scalable ways of giving advice. You can set aside 15 or 30 minutes a week to offer "virtual office hours" wherein you allow aspiring founders to submit questions to you via social media. You can use in-app Q&A functions, or a tool like ngl.link which allows your followers to submit anonymous questions. You can respond to the most commonly asked questions and make your responses available forever as a highlight on your profile so other founders can benefit from your advice.

"When you grow up you tend to get told the world is the way it is and your life is just to live your life inside the world. Try not to bash into the walls too much. Try to have a nice family life, have fun, save a little money. That's a very limited life. Life can be much broader once you discover one simple fact: Everything around you that you call life was made up by people that were no smarter than you. And you can change it, you can influence it... Once you learn that, you'll never be the same again."

— Steve Jobs, Founder of Apple and Pixar

Chapter 8

End of Chapter Summary Checklists

Chapter 2: Preparation
End of Chapter Summary Checklist:

Here is a shortlist of the materials you will need to prepare before you start (some of which you'll continue to iterate on while fundraising):

- ☐ Pitch
- ☐ Fundraising Tracks
- ☐ Outreach Tracking Spreadsheet or CRM
- ☐ Outreach Template Blurb
- ☐ Teaser Deck
- ☐ Full Deck
- ☐ Legal Paperwork
- ☐ Professional Team Headshots

What information to include in a teaser deck:

- ☐ Slide #1: Company Name & Tagline
- ☐ Slide #2: Team
- ☐ Slide #3: Problem / Opportunity
- ☐ Slide #4: Market
- ☐ Slide #5: Why Now
- ☐ Slide #6: Solution (Your Product)
- ☐ Slide #7: Company name and CEO's email address

What information to include in a full deck:

- ☐ Slide #1: Company Name & Tagline
- ☐ Slide #2: Team
- ☐ Slide #3: Problem / Opportunity

- ☐ Slide #4: Solution (Your Product)
- ☐ Slide #5: Why Now
- ☐ Slide #6: How It Works (how your product or service works)
- ☐ Slide #7: Defensibility
- ☐ Slide #8: Traction
- ☐ Slide #9: Vision Statement
- ☐ Slide #10: Company name and CEO's email address

Chapter 3: The Pitch Conversation End of Chapter Summary Checklist:

The Pitch Conversation:

- ☐ Script for setting up the call for success memorized.
- ☐ Questions for the specific investor.
- ☐ Introduction: Introducing yourself, sharing your background, and why you are the right person to build this company.
- ☐ The Problem: Articulate the problem you are trying to solve, how you encountered it, and how many people have this problem (the market).
- ☐ Your Solution (Service or Product): Share a clear one-liner about what your product is or will be, and then share more about how it works from the user's perspective.
- ☐ Why Now: Why this exact moment in time has unlocked this opportunity. Is there a breakthrough new technology that allows this problem to be solved now, when it hasn't been able to be solved in the past? Is there a major societal shift in behavior or change in government laws?
- ☐ Your fundraising tracks for various parts of your business.

Virtual Meetings and Calls Setup: Have a Plan A & Plan B

- ☐ Plan A
    - ☐ Use a computer, laptop, or camera and keep it stable on a desk.
    - ☐ Use high quality internet in your area.
- ☐ Plan B
    - ☐ Use your phone and a phone stand on a desk.
    - ☐ Use high quality cell service in your area.

Chapter 4: Strategy End of Chapter Summary Checklist:

High-Level Fundraising Strategy:

- ☐ Weeks 1-3: Research and outreach
- ☐ Create investor CRM
- ☐ Utilize outreach and follow up templates
- ☐ Week 4: Meetings with venture-backed founders
- ☐ Week 5: Meetings with angels & solo capitalists (AKA quick decision makers) Third tier → First Tier
- ☐ Week 6: Third tier funds
- ☐ Week 7: Second tier funds
- ☐ Week 8: Top tier funds

Fundraising Strategy CRM Preparation:

- ☐ Research and create a list of 3rd tier, 2nd tier, and top tier funds investors.
- ☐ Research each fund, and choose a partner (a GP).
- ☐ Look at your top tier VC investor partner portfolios, and research (news, social media posts, etc.) and find which portfolio founders are their 'golden childs' i.e. favorites. Make a list of those favorite founders.

- ☐ Look at those founders' early-stage raises, and note which angels invested in those companies.
- ☐ Make a list of angels who've invested in your category (consumer, B2B, CPG, etc.).
- ☐ Create a list of founders, top angels & investors on social media and turn on alerts for those specific people.
- ☐ Carve time blocks out in your calendar 2-3X a week to engage with these people on social media. Reshare podcasts these people are featured in, news articles, reshare their blog posts, etc. with nice and thoughtful comments.
- ☐ Create an online presence. Twitter and LinkedIn matter the most for raising.
- ☐ Make a list of your competitors, and a list of VCs and angels that invested in them. Note that you need to ask if there's a conflict.

Chapter 9

Recommended Reading

Founders often reach out to me and ask for book recommendations to help them in their entrepreneurial journey. I typically share 1-3 book suggestions, but always feel I'm forgetting far more useful books than I'm recommending.

In the hope of providing a far better and more comprehensive answer moving forward, below I've included some of the various books I've read and found valuable along my startup journey. Each of these recommendations changed how I think in a meaningful way or helped me move the needle forward as an entrepreneur.

MANAGING YOURSELF

Grit: The Power Of Passion And Perseverance by Angela Duckworth

The Almanack Of Naval Ravikant: A Guide To Wealth And Happiness by Eric Jorgenson

Good Morning, I Love You: Mindfulness And Self-Compassion Practices To Rewire Your Brain For Calm, Clarity, And Joy by Shauna Shapiro

Option B: Facing Adversity, Building Resilience, And Finding Joy by Adam Grant and Sheryl Sandberg

Hidden Genius: The Secret Ways Of Thinking That Power The World's Most Successful People by Polina Marinova Pompliano

Fair Play: A Game-Changing Solution For When You Have Too Much To Do by Eve Rodsky

LifePass: Drop Your Limits, Rise To Your Potential—A Groundbreaking Approach To Goal Setting by Payal Kadakia

The Great CEO Within: The Tactical Guide To Company Building by Matt Mochary

Burn Rate: Launching A Startup And Losing My Mind
by Andy Dunn

Undaunted: Overcoming Doubts And Doubters by Kara Goldin

Big Friendship: How We Keep Each Other Close by Aminatou Sow and Ann Friedman

Belong: Find Your People, Create Community, And Live A More Connected Life by Radha Agrawal

Tools Of Titans: The Tactics, Routines, And Habits Of Billionaires, Icons, And World-Class Performers by Tim Ferriss

CREATING A BETTER WORLD

A Life On Our Planet: My Witness Statement And A Vision For The Future by David Attenborough

So You Want To Talk About Race by Iljeoma Oluo

Wordslut: A Feminist Guide To Taking Back The English Language by Amanda Montell

White Feminism: From The Suffragettes To Influencers And Who They Leave Behind by Koa Beck

Dear White Women: Let's Get (Un)comfortable Talking About Racism by Sara Blanchard and Misasha Suzuki Graham

Brotopia: Breaking Up The Boys' Club Of Silicon Valley by Emily Chang

A Uterus Is A Feature, Not A Bug: The Working Woman's Guide To Overthrowing The Patriarchy by Sarah Lacy

Reset: My Fight For Inclusion And Lasting Change by Ellen Pao

Me And White Supremacy: Combat Racism, Change The World, And Become A Good Ancestor by Layla F. Saad and Robin DiAngelo

How To Be Successful Without Hurting Men's Feelings: Non-Threatening Leadership Strategies For Women by Sarah Cooper

Screaming On The Inside: The Unsustainability Of American Motherhood by Jessica Grose

Whistleblower: My Journey To Silicon Valley And Fight For Justice At Uber by Susan Fowler

BUILDING PRODUCT

The Mom Test by Rob Fitzpatrick

Obviously Awesome: How To Nail Product Positioning So Customers Get It, Buy It, Love It by April Dunford

Hooked: How to Build Habit-Forming Products by Nir Eyal

Build: An Unorthodox Guide To Making Things Worth Making by Tony Fadell

Make Something Wonderful: Steve Jobs In His Own Words by Steve Jobs

Founders At Work: Stories Of Startups' Early Days by Jessica Livingston

The Cold Start Problem: How To Start And Scale Network Effects by Andrew Chen

Exit Path: How To Win The Startup End Game by Touraj Parang

Get Together: How To Build A Community With Your People by Bailey Richardson, Kai Elmer Sotto, and Kevin Huynh

The Lean Product Playbook: How To Innovate With Minimum Viable Products And Rapid Customer Feedback by Dan Olsen

How I Built This: The Unexpected Paths To Success From The World's Most Inspiring Entrepreneurs by Guy Raz

LEADING OTHERS AND COMPANY BUILDING

Let My People Go Surfing: The Education Of A Reluctant Businessman by Yvon Chouinard

Supermaker: Crafting Business On Your Own Terms by Jaime Schmidt

The Ride Of A Lifetime: Lessons Learned From 15 Years As CEO Of The Walt Disney Company by Bob Iger

Nonviolent Communication: Life-Changing Tools For Healthy Relationships by Marshall B. Rosenberg, PhD

Say What You Mean: A Mindful Approach To Nonviolent Communication by Oren Jay Sofer

Who: The A Method For Hiring by Geoff Smart and Randy Street

The Hard Thing About Hard Things: Building A Business When There Are No Easy Answers by Ben Horowitz

High Growth Handbook: Scaling Startups From 10 to 10,000 People by Elad Gil

An Elegant Puzzle: Systems Of Engineering Management by Will Larson

The Minimalist Entrepreneur: How Great Founders Do More With Less by Sahil Lavingia

The 15 Commitments Of Conscious Leadership: A New Paradigm For Sustainable Success by Jim Dethmer

How To Build A Goddamn Empire: Advice On Creating Your Brand With High-Tech Smarts, Elbow Grease, Infinite Hustle, And A Whole Lotta Heart by Ali Kriegsman

Shoe Dog: A Memoir By The Creator Of Nike by Phil Knight

The Power Of Ritual: How To Create Meaning And Connection In Everything You Do by Casper ter Kuile

The Making Of A Manager: What To Do When Everyone Looks To You by Julie Zhuo

Powerful: Building A Culture Of Freedom And Responsibility by Patty McCord

FUNDRAISING MECHANICS

Venture Deals: Be Smarter Than Your Lawyer And Venture Capitalist by Brad Feld and Jason Mendelson

Backable: The Surprising Truth Behind What Makes People Take A Chance On You by Suneel Gupta

Secrets Of Sand Hill Road: Venture Capital And How To Get It by Scott Kupor

The Power Law: Venture Capital And The Making Of The New Future by Sebastian Mallaby

Valley Speak: Deciphering the Jargon of Silicon Valley by Rochelle Kopp and Steven Ganz

SILICON VALLEY HISTORY & CULTURE

Valley Of Genius: The Uncensored History Of Silicon Valley by Adam Fisher

Palo Alto: A History Of California, Capitalism, And The World by Malcolm Harris

Troublemakers: Silicon Valley's Coming Of Age by Leslie Berlin

The Contrarian: Peter Thiel And Silicon Valley's Pursuit Of Power by Max Chafkin

Uncanny Valley: A Memoir by Anna Wiener

Bad Blood: Secrets And Lies In A Silicon Valley Startup by John Carreyrou

Glossary

Accelerator: An organization designed to help startups grow and scale through mentorship, funding, and resources.

Acquisition: When one company purchases most or all of another company's shares to gain control of that company.

Advisory Board: A group of individuals selected to provide expert advice and guidance to a company but without formal legal responsibilities.

Alpha: A measure of an investment's performance on a risk-adjusted basis.

Angel Investor: An individual who provides capital for a business startup, usually in exchange for convertible debt or ownership equity.

Back-channeling: Covert or unofficial communication between parties.

Beta: A measure of the volatility of a stock or portfolio compared to the overall market.

Blue-chip investors: Investors who are reputable, well-established, and have a history of stable earnings.

Board of Directors: A group of people who jointly oversee the activities of an organization.

Bootstrapping: Starting and growing a business without external funding or investment.

Burn Rate: The rate at which a company is spending its capital.

Capitalization Table: A table providing an analysis of a company's percentages of ownership, equity dilution, and value of equity in each round of investment.

Customer Acquisition Cost: The cost associated with convincing a customer to buy a product/service.

De Novo Capital: The portion of VC capital that they use for their very first investment.

Demo Day: An event where startups present their business ideas to a large audience, typically consisting of investors.

Down Round: Getting lower valuations in the next round of financing.

Due Diligence: An investigation or audit of a potential investment or product.

Equity: Ownership interest in a corporation in the form of stock or shares.

Exit Strategy: A planned approach to liquidating an investor's stake in a business.

FAANG Company: An acronym representing five prominent American technology companies including Facebook (now known as Meta), Apple, Amazon, Netflix, and Alphabet (formerly known as Google).

Follow-On Capital: VC capital kept in reserve to maintain ownership in their companies in subsequent rounds.

Friends and Family: An early round of business financing from close personal connections.

Growth Hacking: Strategies focused solely on business growth, often unconventional.

Hot round: A financing round in which a startup's valuation increases rapidly.

Initial Public Offering (IPO): The first time a company's stock is offered to the public.

Iterate: To make repeated versions of a product or process, improving it each time.

Limited Partner (LP): An investor in a partnership who has limited liability and is not involved in day-to-day management.

Merger: A combination of two companies to form a new company.

Monetization: The process of converting something into money.

NDA (Non-Disclosure Agreement): A legally binding contract that prevents someone from sharing confidential information.

Network Effects: The effect that one user of a good or service has on the value of that product to others.

Pain Point: A specific problem that potential customers of your business are experiencing.

Party Round: A funding round where numerous investors each contribute relatively small sums of money.

Pitch: A presentation given by a startup or entrepreneur to potential investors.

Positioning: The way a product is presented to and perceived by its target market.

Product Market Fit: The degree to which a product satisfies a strong market demand.

Prototype: An early sample or model built to test a concept or process.

Scalability: The ability of a business or system to grow without being hampered by its structure or available resources.

Stealth Mode: When a startup company operates in secret to protect its business ideas and technology.

Stock Options: Contracts that grant the holder the right to buy or sell a stock at a specific price.

Syndicate: A group of investors who pool their resources to invest together.

Take Rate: The percentage of transactions a company earns revenue on.

Term Sheet: A non-binding agreement outlining the basic terms and conditions for an investment.

Total Addressable Market: The total market demand for a product or service.

Unicorn: A privately-held startup company valued at over $1 billion.

User Experience: The overall experience of a person using a product, especially in terms of how easy or pleasing it is to use.

Venture Capitalist: An investor who either provides capital to startup ventures or supports small companies that wish to expand.

Vesting: The process by which an employee earns rights to company stock over time.

Vertical: Refers to a specific industry or market they're targeting.

Virality: The quality or fact of being shared widely as a piece of content, especially on social media.

Portfolio: A collection of investments held by an investment company, hedge fund, financial institution, or individual.

Notes

Chapter 1: Introduction

1. Gornall, Will, and Ilya A. Strebulaev. "The Economic Impact of Venture Capital: Evidence from Public Companies." SSRN, June 2021, https://ssrn.com/abstract=2681841 or http://dx.doi.org/10.2139/ssrn.2681841.
2. Tamaseb, Ali. *Super Founders: What Data Reveals About Billion-Dollar Startups.* PublicAffairs, 2021.
3. National Venture Capital Association. *2019 Yearbook.* 2019, https://nvca.org/wp-content/uploads/2019/08/NVCA-2019-Yearbook.pdf.
4. "The Economic Impact of Venture Capital: Evidence from Public Companies." *Stanford Graduate School of Business*, 1 Nov. 2015, www.gsb.stanford.edu/faculty-research/working-papers/economic-impact-venture-capital-evidence-public-companies.

Chapter 2: Preparation

1. Renbarger, Madeline. "Pitch-Deck Library: Search Over 1050 Pitch Decks That Startups Including Uber, Postmates, and Airbnb Used to Raise Millions." *Business Insider*, Business Insider, www.businessinsider.com/searchable-database-of-business-insider-pitch-decks-2020-7. Accessed 4 June 2023.
2. Pollan, Michael. Food Rules: *An Eater's Manual.* Penguin Books, 2013.
3. Walker, Matthew. *Why We Sleep.* Scribner, 2017.
4. "Manta Sleep Mask - Because Better Sleep Unlocks Your Best Life." *Manta Sleep*, mantasleep.com/. Accessed 4 Sept. 2023.
5. Attia, Peter. "Alcohol, Sleep, and Stress: A Self-Fulfilling Prophecy." *Peter Attia*, 31 Mar. 2022, peterattiamd.com/alcohol-sleep-and-stress/.

6. Attia, Peter. Outlive: *The Science & Art of Longevity*. Penguin Random House USA, 2023.

Chapter 3: The Pitch Conversation

1. Oluo, Ijeoma. *So You Want to Talk About Race*. Seal Press, 2019.
2. Shapiro, Shauna. *Rewiring Your Mind*. Sounds True, 2022.
3. Voss, Chris, and Tahl Raz. *Never Split the Difference: Negotiating As If Your Life Depended On It*. HarperBusiness, 2016.

Chapter 5: Managing Yourself

1. Freeman, Michael A. "Are Entrepreneurs 'Touched with Fire'?" *Are Entrepreneurs Touched With Fire?*, UC Berkeley, 17 Apr. 2015, michaelafreemanmd.com/Research_files/Are%20Entrepreneurs%20 Touched%20with%20Fire%20(pre-pub%20n)%204-17-15.pdf.
2. Dutton, Kevin. The Wisdom of Psychopaths: *What Saints, Spies, and Serial Killers Can Teach Us About Success*. Scientific American / Farrar, Straus and Giroux, 2013.
3. "Psychopathy." Edited by Psychology Today Staff, *Psychology Today*, Sussex Publishers, www.psychologytoday.com/us/basics/psychopathy. Accessed 1 Aug. 2023.
4. Croom, Simon. "Commentary: 12% of Corporate Leaders Are Psychopaths. It's Time to Take This Problem Seriously." *Fortune*, Fortune, 6 June 2021, fortune.com/2021/06/06/corporate-psychopaths-business-leadership-csr/.
5. 18. Cuddy, Amy. "Your Body Language May Shape Who You Are." *TED Talk*, 1 June 2012, https://www.ted.com/talks/amy_cuddy_ your_body_language_may_shape_who_you_are?language=en. Accessed 1 July 2023.
6. Mochary, Matt. "Parenting as a CEO." Mocharymethod.Com, mocharymethod.com/. Accessed 1 June 2023.
7. Grind, Kirsten, and Katherine Bindley. "Magic Mushrooms. LSD. Ketamine. The Drugs That Power Silicon Valley." *The Wall Street Journal*, Dow Jones & Company, 27 June 2023, www.wsj.com/ articles/silicon-valley-microdosing-ketamine-lsd-magic-mushrooms-d381e214.

8. Huberman, Andrew. "What Alcohol Does to Your Body, Brain & Health." *Huberman Lab*, 22 Aug. 2022, hubermanlab.com/what-alcohol-does-to-your-body-brain-health/.

9. Whitaker, Holly. *Quit like A Woman: The Radical Choice to Not Drink in a Culture Obsessed with Alcohol.* The Dial Press, 2021.

10. "American Time Use Survey Tables Page." *U.S. Bureau of Labor Statistics*, U.S. Bureau of Labor Statistics, www.bls.gov/tus/tables.htm. Accessed 1 Mar. 2023.

11. Goldsmith, Annie. "The Brain-Body Investment Survey: What 500 Subscribers Are Spending to Boost Their Performance." *The Information*, The Information, 28 Aug. 2023,

12. Attia, Peter. *Reduce Your All Cause Mortality By 50%. YouTube*, YouTube, 5 June 2023, https://www.youtube.com/shorts/Y8hOn-2F2xRA. Accessed 4 Sept. 2023.

Acknowledgements

I never could have written this book without the steady support, love, advice and inspiration provided by my family, Russ, Cynthia, and Sarah Leibson. Thank you for always believing in me, my dreams, and your editing help all of my life. I wish grandma and grandpa were here to read this and I miss them.

Martin, my best friend and husband—thank you for enduring the entire writing journey by my side without a single complaint. You are the best dad. Adrian, by the time you read this, I hope you understand that I write because I want a better world and the brightest future for you. You both bring me so much joy and happiness, and I'm grateful for each and every moment I have with you.

I owe a huge debt of gratitude to my tireless, unstoppable team at Jetpack Books and so many folks that helped me along the way of making this book a reality. Thank you Diana Ang, Karina Granda, Sarah Lacy, Paul Bradley Carr, and so many more.

I'm also eternally grateful to so many people for their support, kindness, and time spent helping me including Tom Kosnik, Alex Pall, Sarah Cooper, Lenny Rachitsky, Luba Yudasina, Nir Eyal, Shauna Shapiro, Ali Kriegsman, Steve Blank, Jason Feifer, Jamie Schmidt, Vivian Tu, Jaclyn Johnson, Amanda Montell, and Alisson Wood.

I'm eternally grateful for everyone that has believed in me and supported my startup journey including Jessica Livingston, Leonardo DiCaprio, Kat Manalac, Adam D'Angelo, Andrew Chen, Jeremy LaTrasse, Kimbal Musk, Ha Nguyen, Christina Li, 24kGoldn, Leslie Schrock, and many more.

For their friendship, advice, support, and encouragement I also want to thank Mary Hubert, the Levihn family, Hayley Taitz, Tina Edwards, Morgan Tardy, Ava and Mark Michiels, Brittany Guilleaume, Aris Andros, Jesse Andros, Erika Veurink, Lauren Graves, Moritz Niendorf, and Amy Kao.

Finally, I want to thank you, Dear Reader, for coming along this adventure with me. Please send me a note to @hayleyleibson and share what you are building.

Hayley Leibson
Mill Valley, California
December 19, 2023

About the Author

HAYLEY LEIBSON is a venture-backed startup founder, award-winning product leader, and writer with deep expertise in consumer technology and artificial intelligence. She's a Forbes 30 Under 30 alum and Board Member, Y Combinator alum, and a *Silicon Valley Business Journal* "Woman of Influence." Hayley co-founded the $100 million-dollar a16z-backed startup Lunchclub, the world's first AI superconnector that connects millions of people globally for jobs, mentorship, and more. She is an advocate for inclusion and diversity in the technology industry, and her work has been featured in *The Wall Street Journal, ABC, Harper's Bazaar, The Washington Post*, and many more. "Raise Early Stage Venture Capital: The First Guide to Startup Fundraising for Women and Minority Founders" is her first book. She lives in Mill Valley, California with her husband and baby boy.

www.ingramcontent.com/pod-product-compliance
Lightning Source LLC
Chambersburg PA
CBHW051623010526
44119CB00040B/486/J